# LING'RING MEM'RIES

## CAROLINE F. STEVENS

*Bless you,*

*Caroline F. Stevens*

# A NOTE FROM THE AUTHOR

This book is in memory of my beloved husband, Herman C. Stevens, "Pappy," as we called him. The sale proceeds will be given to First Christian Church, Columbia, SC, as was the case with my previous books:

Fragments of Love, 1980
A Stowaway's Heritage, 1985
Digging Wells, 1987
Love's Legacy, 1996

# THANK YOU!

A thank you is due to my daughter
Who worked so diligently on this book,
Typing and typing and typing some more.
Both of us weary, we wanted a nook
Without periods or commas or even a rhyme;
Just give us some space.
Give us some time!

Thank you, Christina,
For another labor of love!


My gratefulness is also expressed to my other
family members and to my church family.
Thank you and God bless you.

# FOREWORD

W e are told that "a picture is worth a thousand words." Images, still or moving, have come to be one of the foremost ways in which people communicate. Even those mediums of the printed word, newspapers and magazines, often rely on photographs to add weight to the words wielded by writers. The computer connected to the World Wide Web, brings us more picture communication daily.

How difficult then the task of the poet. One who paints pictures with words alone? The poet must communicate a beautiful scene to us so that it comes alive in our minds, without the aid of pictures. Add to that task the meter and rhyme each poem must follow.

Yet poets not only embrace this challenge, they excel with the style! Poetry not only communicates pictures, events, and descriptions; it is able to share emotions, thoughts and spiritual matters. Where prose and pictures are left hanging to describe the "unseen," the poet is able to continue charting the unexplored.

Such an explorer is Caroline Stevens. The words she uses in *Ling'ring Mem'ries* reach out into our world and tell us of that which we see, but cannot voice. Her words explore the depth of human emotion and thought, where the camera or the paintbrush offer no help in the attempt to record or interpret. The verse she writes is alive with an awareness and appreciation of God's Spirit which surrounds us all. She is able to do this because she is a very observant person, taking in more than just that which meets the eye. She is a sensitive, emotional, and loving person. She is a spiritual person, who daily walks in awareness of God's will.

She speaks in the language of poetry, surely a spiritual gift from God. Enjoy these interpretations of the world and human beings as spoken by the poet. Let her show you that which camera and pictures cannot.

Rev. F. Torrance Osgood
April 2010

# CONTENTS

❧

## LING'RING MEM'RIES

In the springtime of our lives
Perhaps we're not aware
Of the mem'ries we are making
To become like jewels rare.

But when our age is golden
And our days are hastening on
How we hallow precious mem'ries
Of days now past and gone.

We frame them in our hearts
And forever they will be
The tie of love and friendship
Beckoning to Eternity.


January 13, 2007

# FAITH

Faith is the substance of things hoped for,
The evidence of things we can't see.
This is the teaching of Paul,
Indeed it seems like a mystery.

Jesus reaches down to each one of us,
And if we believe, we also can behold....
Step by step His Holy Spirit
Will guide us to the Fold!

## WHAT FAITH CAN DO

Faith can move those mountains
Of fear and doubt, distrust,
When we draw apart with Jesus,
And listen, yes, we must.

Faith can show us heaven
And His mysterious ways
When we give to Him our burdens
And serve Him all our days.

Faith can make the difference
In who we really are,
A slow and dismal creature,
Or a bright and shining star.

Faith will win our vict'ries.
Ah, faith will see us through!
As the planted bulb discovers life,
We, too, will find what faith can do!

## GOD IS LISTENING

God is always listening,
Waiting for our prayers.
He knows our trials and temptations;
Oh yes, He knows and cares!

He'll grant us strength upon request;
He'll hold us in His arms.
And we can climb the mountain tops,
Secure from all alarms.

When we stand with Jesus
We'll know from day to day
He lifts; He loves; He listens
And leads us all the way!

## WELLS OF STRENGTH

When we have found the Messiah
We're never quite the same.
He makes of us new persons
Without a change of name.

He gives us clearer vision
To behold and truly see
Things of beauty all around us,
Which He made for you and me.

He helps us find our places,
To use each talent and skill,
And we grow in the gentle process
As we bend to His Holy Will.

We find wells of strength within us
To do what He'd have us do.
We no longer say, "I don't have time,"
For each day we love Him anew.

When we have found the Messiah
We find these words to be true:
"A new heart also will I give....
A new spirit will I put within you."

## WILL YOU BE CLAY?

Will you be clay
For the Master's hands,
Yielding yourself to his call,
Feeling the power
Of the spirit within
Stir to the voice so small?

Will you become
What he wants you to be,
Growing and reaching toward him;
Loving and lifting
And tending his sheep,
Being a shepherd to them?

Will you be there
When he needs you most
To tell what he's done for you?
Will you follow his leading,
Rejoice in achieving,
Praise him for life anew!

July 2000

## EARTHEN VESSELS

We are earthen vessels
But in our hands we hold
A gift that is more precious
Than earth's silver and its gold.

We are earthen vessels,
Made from the Master's mold,
To serve in the Master's vineyard,
Whether we be young or old.

We are earthen vessels,
Fashioned of fragile clay,
Given a mighty mission,
To change, to lead, to sway.

We are earthen vessels
To be filled and to overflow
With the healing love of Jesus;
That a broken world may know.

## THE SHOES MY SAVIOR WORE

The shoes my Savior wore
Upon His dusty feet
Tell a story, oh, so tender,
Tell a story, oh, so sweet.
They speak of love and understanding,
And patience, too, to bear
The crosses of this life with vic'try,
And not with gloom and fear!

They tell of little boys and girls
Who sat upon His knee,
Smiling, I'm sure, when Jesus said,
"Let the children come to me."
They tell of her who pressed the crowds
To see His gentle face,
To touch His garment and, behold,
To know His saving grace!

They tell of those who listened
And learned from Him to live.
Yea, the message of the ages
Has been theirs to share and give.
His shoes speak of salvation,
They speak of sorrow, too;
How He climbed the hills of Calvary,
Where He died for me and you!

Will you wear the shoes of Jesus
On your tired and dusty feet?
Will you know a lasting friendship
That will make your life complete?
Will you walk the roads with Jesus;
Will you serve Him in your day?
You will find each hour a blessing
As you follow in His way!

## MIRRORS OF GOD'S LOVE

We're mirrors of your love, Father,
Reflecting what we see
In the face of Jesus,
Who cares so tenderly.

We're candles in a dark world, Father;
You've set us all aglow
To bear the message of salvation
'Til all the world shall know

You're our Peace and Joy, Father,
And strength for all our days.
With us, in us, through us;
Your love will shine always.

Yes, you can use us all, Father,
When we give our lives to Thee.
With eyes always on Jesus
Ours is the Victory!

December 19, 2006

## TO BE A SHEPHERD

To be a shepherd is an awesome thing.
It reaches back to Biblical days,
And brings to mind those early Christians;
Making us aware in so many ways
How they loved each other;
How they helped each other;
How they shared the message of Christ!

Lydia was such a shepherd.
Down by the river she met with her flock.
They sang together;
They prayed together,
And they shared the message of Christ!

Now I am your appointed shepherd.
I want to help you if I can.
We're extending a special invitation
For you to worship with us each Lord's day.
Let's sing together;
Let's pray together;
Let's share the message of Christ!


March 2005

## SHARED FAITH

Once upon a time,
And many years ago,
A teacher whom I loved
Helped me to learn and grow.
She taught more than curriculum;
She shared her faith with me.
A strong, courageous Christian;
Like her I vowed to be!

Brighten the corner where you are
And lend a helping hand.
Just pass the love of Jesus
So others may understand.
Simple though they sound,
These words ring very true;
When applied to daily living
Miracles can happen to me and you!

Yes, talents lie within us
For God has put them there,
But they must be cultivated
If fruit for Him we'd bear.
We must reach out to others
And share our faith in love;
And praise God for the blessings
He sends from heaven above!

Believers do not hibernate;
They communicate with each other,
Thereby giving spiritual strength
To help a weaker brother.
Each one of us becomes a teacher,
Touching lives in different ways.
Like flowers, we bloom for Jesus.
May He bless us all our days!

April 13, 1997
Written for Spiritual Awakening promotion

## GROWING UP INTO CHRIST

When I was a child
I looked to my earthly parents
For guidance and love, like you,
But when I became a Christian
It was as though I was born anew;
Aware of my heavenly Father,
His world, His word,
All His promises true.

The way has not always been easy;
There've been trials and problems, too,
But Jesus has always helped me,
Just as He said He would do.
Together we've walked in His garden,
Where flowers of friendship grow
And I feel the warmth of His presence
In the faces I've come to know.

Many have been my teachers;
And perhaps, I've taught a few;
But sharing and caring have been the core.
It's the reason I love you and you.
I praise God for all of His children
As we grow in His grace each day,
As we work and we worship together,
Finding joy that will last us for aye.

The jewels of this world cannot lure us;
There are brighter ones by far
In that home we have in Heaven,
Where the gates are always ajar.
As the years slip away into history,
And our steps become somewhat slow,
Be it known our hearts are singing,
"In Christ we live and thrive and grow!"

April 25, 1999
Spiritual Awakening

## TO US HE'S EVERYTHING

As Disciples we are learners
Seeking truth for each new day,
Listening for His still small voice,
Finding courage to obey.

As Disciples we are disciplined
To prioritize our lives,
To put God first in everything,
Receiving blessings in disguise.

As Disciples we must answer
To a high and mighty King.
We serve Him for we love Him
And to us He's everything.

He's Peace on earth and joy complete,
He's happiness without end.
And all because He simply said,
"If you'll be my Disciples
I will be your Friend."

## WE DRINK TO YOUR REMEMBRANCE

Today, our Father, as we drink
From this symbolic cup,
We remember it was with love
Your dear Son filled it up.
It was with love He lived
And died on Calvary's tree;
To heal our wounds of sin
And make us clean and free.

He has invited us to come
And often sup with Him.
This is another Upper Room;
The lights are low and dim.
And He is here in spirit
As on that precious day,
To challenge and renew us,
To send us on our way!

Dear Jesus, bless and keep us
Within Your loving fold.
We drink to Your remembrance,
To the greatest story ever told:
The story of how love
Came through the mire of human dross,
And claimed for us the victory
Of the dear old rugged cross!

1980

## PARTNERS WITH GOD

We are called to be God's partners,
Each in his own time and way;
Using gifts bestowed upon us,
Digging wells for our day.

We are called to be God's partners;
Ah, what a call divine,
But how am I to answer
Unless Thy will is mine.

Drop the baggage you are carrying
And follow after me,
And be a faithful servant
Until Eternity.

You cannot change the whole world
But there's something you can do.
Be a blessing where you are
And to your God be true.

Dig a well to leave behind
As you travel this old sod.
Another thirsting soul may drink;
Be a partner too with God.

## GEMSTONES

Five little stones were given to me
To help me remember a special day.
Now I share their story with you,
For it's helped me along my way.

The first stone represents prayer,
Something I can't live without.
For whatever task I'm attempting to do
I must feel He approves of what I'm about.

The second stone represents zeal.
Yes, enthusiasm is what we need.
Catch the spirit and pass it on;
Even a smile can become a seed.

The third stone represents work,
An ethic I learned as a child.
Certainly a leader must set the course,
Delegating, delighting, not bossy and wild.

The fourth stone represents love,
The glue that binds us together,
Making our tasks seem like fun,
Yes, making us friends forever.

The fifth stone represents joy,
A bi-product of all that we do.
A time to rejoice in what we accomplish,
A time to thank God for helping us too!

March 2004

## UNEXPECTED

In an unexpected manner
Jesus came to earth one day,
As a baby in a manger,
Unexpected, there He lay.
But the heavens rang with gladness
On the night that He was born,
And men down through the ages
Still His Name with praise adorn!

In an unexpected manner
Jesus grew to be a man,
Not a prince with worldly riches,
But with power that could command
Unexpected things to happen.
Yea, the world has never known
Such miracles as were wrought by Him,
Such kindness as was sown.

In an unexpected manner
Jesus left the earth one day,
Crucified by those He loved
In a humiliating way.
Yet the story that He gave us
Is the one that can not die.
'Tis the faith of every Christian
And a trust to hold it high!

In an unexpected manner
Jesus walks the earth again,
And we see Him as we witness,
As we strive to stamp out sin.
We feel His power within us
As we serve Him day by day.
And we share a joy with those
Who've walked this unexpected way!

## THE LIGHT WE WALK IN

The light we walk in
Encircles the globe,
Each weary traveler
Wears a shining robe.
No matter the color
Or texture of skin;
One Heavenly Father,
We all are akin.

The light we walk in
Comes down from above;
'Tis known as no other
Than God's holy love.
'Twas born in a manger
And hung on a cross,
But a vic'try was won;
A gain, not a loss!

The light we walk in
Must never grow dim.
Remember the footsteps
That were made by Him.
"Go tell them," He says,
"I died for them, too."
How can we do less
And to Him be true!

## THE HUMANITY OF HAITI

It was just another summer day,
Children ling'ring at their play;
Seagulls watching o'er the shores,
People busy with their chores.

In a flash their world was changed
By a quake whose horror ranged
High on the scale of history,
Leaving a gruesome sight to see.

Homes, once havens, turned to rubble,
Burying loved ones, causing trouble.
Nowhere to go but on the street,
No water to drink, no food to eat.

Desperate, homeless, hurting are they
Who're left to tell of that fateful day;
But with our help they will survive.
Thank God that we are all alive!

Give from your heart and give today.
For the humanity of Haiti let us pray!

January 20, 2010

## WEEK OF COMPASSION

Week of Compassion is a wonderful ministry;
It helps people everywhere,
Reflecting the love of Jesus Christ,
Showing the world Disciples care.

Week of Compassion has lofty goals,
Not tied to a certain date.
Who knew the tsunami would strike when it did?
Who knew the extent and its victims' fate?

Who knew that a hurricane of terrible force
Would leave thousands without a home?
When it happens so quickly
One must feel helpless, bereft and alone.

Floods and famines, poverty too,
All come in their own time.
Just thank God with all your heart
If they do not alter your life and mine.

Continue to give to this ministry
That's prepared and ready to serve
To the ends of the earth for Jesus sake:
A mission from which it won't swerve!

February 2005

## GIFTS OF LIVING WATER

Our offerings to Week of Compassion
Are like gifts of living water,
Flowing out with a message of love.
They speak of the Christ within us,
Praising God with the angels above!
They provide help for the hurting
Wherever in the world they may be,
To hurricane survivors in North Carolina
Or our sisters and brothers across the sea.

Irrigation systems, education systems,
Blankets for a cold refugee;
Wells of pure drinking water;
They help the oppressed go free.
Grain for drought stricken farmers,
Pastoral and medical care,
Food for malnourished children;
They scatter God's love everywhere.

I like to think our gifts might touch
A poor, lonely girl or boy,
Changing the picture we often see
From hopelessness, fear and poverty
To a glimmer of light, opportunity.
It's within our power; we can and we must
Make a difference as we go our way.
Share the precious gifts of living water;
Be a blessing and be blessed today!

February 2000
Week of Compassion

## MANY PLACES CALL US

Many places call us, Lord,
To be your witness there;
Many faces greet us, Lord,
Some dark, some brown, some fair.

We see you in each setting
Extend your nail-pierced hand
That all might know compassion
And some might understand.

We see the Chinese youth, Lord,
Whose dream is to be free
And know the joy of living
In a Christian democracy.

We see the power that binds them
In slavery to its will,
And we pray the shackles may be broken
And Christ their hearts may fill.

Many places call us, Lord,
To be your hands and feet.
Walk with us on our journey, Lord,
Until in Heaven we meet!

February 8, 1993

## HELPING THE UNFORTUNATES

You don't have to go to Africa
To find what hunger means.
You don't have to be a refugee
To yearn for rice and beans.

You don't have to be a street person
To be without a home.
Just lose your job and pretty soon
You may find you'll have to roam.

It happens here; it happens there;
It happens everywhere.
Families are suffering
Much more than they can bear.

That's why our Family Shelter,
And other helpers too,
Reach out in love and understanding
To say, "We care for you."

They lift up those who've fallen;
They try to meet each need.
They work toward permanent solutions,
Reflecting Christ in word and deed!

February 28, 1988
Written for Week of Compassion

## BY HIS GRACE

By His grace I stand before you
On this beautiful Lord's day.
I am here again for Missions;
And this is what I want to say.
Our Easter offering serves people,
Sharing God's transforming love;
It helps us see our risen Savior
And hear His message from Above.

You are my disciples;
You are my hands and feet.
I send you out to care for my flock,
To hear the stories of those you meet.
I need you to build a world with hope,
To share the good news everywhere,
To proclaim my peace that passeth understanding,
To let the little children know I care.

It will take your energy and time
And all that you possibly can give,
But remember the cross and saving grace
And see how abundantly you will live.
By His grace I stand before you
On this beautiful Lord's day
To thank Him for blessing us
Amazingly, Abundantly, Always!

Easter 2004

## LISTEN TO THE CHILDREN

Listen to the children;
Hear the message they impart.
It's filled with expectation,
And it's close to every heart.

Listen to the children;
How wise the little ones are.
They teach us who are their teachers,
And learn easier by far.

Listen to the children.
Reach out a helping hand
To those who need assistance.
True love they understand.

Listen to the children,
And find a glad surprise,
In changing what we can for them,
You'll see sheer joy in their eyes.

Listen to the children.
We have them for today
To mold as God would have us,
Oh, what precious potter's clay!

Written for a devotional presented at CWF-CMF Meeting,
May 17, 1998, when Carolyn Wolff from
Children Unlimited brought the program.

## IT IS THE CHRIST

It is the Christ who calls us
In His compassionate way
To help His little children
Have a safe and brighter day.

It is the Christ who shows us
The reflection of His Face
In each unfortunate one we meet.
Oh, what joy to know His Grace!

It is the Christ who binds us
Into one family,
With a bond of love to keep us
For all eternity.

It is the Christ who warns us,
In words said fittingly,
"If you did it not to the least of these
You did it not to me."

It is this Christ we worship;
It is this Christ we praise.
Then let's serve Him with our actions
And crown Him all our days!

Written for Week of Compassion, 1990

## OPEN OUR EYES

Open our eyes, Lord,
That, seeing, we may see
The world in which we live,
Its yearnings and its agony.

Help us discern the needy,
Not only those in poverty,
But those devoid of learning,
Who lack integrity.

Help us remove the chains,
Whatever they may be
That bind our fellowman;
Let him at last go free.

Help us reflect upon
The reason we are here,
For no matter who we are
To you we're very dear.

Open our eyes, Lord,
That, seeing we may see
Your world, your precious children,
And let us respond accordingly.

## THE POWER OF PENTECOST

Let the power of Pentecost prevail
And fill each heart today.
May it truly lift our spirits,
Lead us gently along life's busy way.

Let the power of Pentecost prevail
As we sing unto a mighty King,
Who sent His Son to be the Messiah.
Proclaim His love. It is a wondrous thing.

Let the power of Pentecost prevail
As we bow our heads in prayer.
Let us listen for that still small voice;
Then go out to show Him that we care.

Let the power of Pentecost prevail
When we commune together at His table.
Remembering the sacrifice that Jesus made
Strengthens our faith and makes us able.

Let the power of Pentecost prevail
As we bring our gifts of love.
We gladly share them that others may know
The joy of salvation and a home in heaven above.


May 30, 2004

## FEED MY SHEEP

I see the gentle Shepherd;
I hear His voice today.
Feed my sheep, I beg you;
Show them salvation's way.

Reach out to the children,
The children of the street;
Give them refreshing water,
The best of all life's treats.

Walk with them to the well
From the desert they now know,
And hold them as they drink
'Til a smile of peace can show.

Restore the magic of their childhood
And teach their lips to pray.
Feed my sheep, my little lambs,
I beg of you today!

May 17, 1998
Written for CWF Devotional

## WHAT WILL WE WRITE?

What will we write upon the pages of this new millennium?
What will we do with each passing day of this new year?
It seems we are a very special people,
Blessed in so many different ways.
Dare we forget who we are and the witness which we hold dear.

As Christian women let's remember
The challenge is for me and you.
To reach out to others in loving friendship,
To study, to learn, to worship and to do;
To pray, to visit, to give most generously;
To reflect the grace of that gracious One
Who died for us on Calvary.

We know in Him we'll find our confidence and hope,
And strength for all the days and tasks to come;
And surely we will write in golden letters
The things that through Him we have gladly done.
God bless you on your journey;
God keep you every one.
Happy New Year, Happy Millennium!

January 1, 2000

## THE PHILIPPINES

The Philippines.
What do they mean to me?
Out there in the vast Pacific
And bordered by the South China Sea.

A cluster of many islands.
We call it archipelago,
But fifty-seven million call it home,
And they love the name Filipino.

Their history has been one of struggle,
Oppression, and poverty too.
Out of untold suffering has come
A culture like an epic true.

They've blended their ancient beliefs
With the Christian tradition they hold.
And from it has been born a people
Who are loyal, courageous and bold.

They've copied some of our customs;
Some dress the American way.
Some come to our country to live
To escape the doom of their day.

Others stay on, preserving the system.
From them we may learn if we will
How love perseveres, with faith enduring,
As it struggles up a steep, rugged hill!


January 10, 1990
Written for presentation of CWF study
on The Philippines, "Rice in the Storm."

## WHAT I LEARNED AT SUNDAY SCHOOL

The simplest lessons I ever learned
I learned at Sunday School.
Etched on my heart they linger
To enhance the meaning of the Golden Rule:
Jesus is the good Shepherd
And we are all his sheep.
He loves all the little children,
And His promises He will keep!

He promises to forgive us
When we bow before God's throne
And confess our sins before Him,
Then set out to atone.
We find His grace and mercy
Are sufficient for each day.
We don't need to ever worry
If our Jesus leads the way!

If we love Him we will serve Him,
And count our blessings too.
There's a joy in my heart
I needs must share with you.
I must tell you of my Savior,
How He died to set me free;
It's a story I cannot keep,
Unmatched love for you and me!

The greatest lessons I ever learned
I learned at Sunday School.
Etched on my heart they linger still
And give new meaning to the Golden Rule.
Teachers may come and teachers may go,
But the lessons remain the same.
God's Word stands forever and ever,
Its truth an eternal flame!

September 14, 1997

## WE ARE HIS DISCIPLES

We are His disciples
In His world today;
Two by two He chooses
And sends us on our way.

He's always there to help us
When we recognize
The lordship of our Master
Through earthly, human eyes.

We feel His strength within us;
We know that inner glow
As we seek to do His will,
To overcome ourselves and grow.

We are His disciples
In His world today
Onward, then and upward;
Let us watch and work and pray!

## LET ME LISTEN WITH MY HEART

Let me listen with my heart, Lord,
As you gently speak to me;
Let me send my light, Lord,
For all the world to see.
Let justice, action, mercy
Take precedence in my life;
Your peace and joy overcome
Misunderstandings and strife.
Replace my weakness with your strength, Lord,
And send me on my way
To join others in the quest, Lord,
Of witnessing today!

Amen.

## ALIVE IN CHRIST

Alive in Christ,
Living to the fullest every day;
Seeking, sharing, praying
That as He calls us we'll obey

Alive in Christ,
Alert to every opportunity;
Reaching, growing, stretching
To the stature He designs for you and me.

Alive in Christ,
And dead to worldly sin;
Thanking, praising, rejoicing
As we let the Savior in.

Alive in Christ,
Who makes our hearts to sing,
Grants us a royal heritage,
And says we're children of a King.

Alive in Christ,
And may it ever be
"Not I that lives," as Paul once said
"But Christ that lives in me."

Written for CWF Group II Meeting,
April 1991, following the CWF study theme,
Alive in Christ.

## DECISIONS, DECISIONS

I can't decide for you;
You can't decide for me,
But God can direct our thinking,
And help us live authentically.

There is a challenge for you;
There is a challenge for me,
We were not made to be wall-flowers;
We're to set the downtrodden free.

We're to give action to our faith,
To share, to lift, and to love,
To feel there's a purpose for living,
And He's ever watching us from above.

It's true I am just one person,
But still I am not alone,
For Jesus always walks with me
And our path is not set in stone.

It leads us in interesting bi-ways,
And, oh, the dear people we meet!
I'm so glad I decided to follow;
My faith has been given new feet!


Written for CWF Retreat 1990

## I'M A CARIBBEAN WOMAN

I'm a Caribbean woman;
My roots go back to slavery,
But I have found a heavenly Father
In my struggle for identity.

He gives me life; He gives me hope.
I raise my hands above.
In rhythmic praise I worship Him,
My God, whose name I love.

I'm a Caribbean woman;
Not rich, perhaps, like you,
But my home is just as precious;
And I find joy in what I do.

I teach my children to be just
And rise above sheer poverty,
But always treasure the gifts we have
In this great land of sky and sea.

I'm a Caribbean woman;
I feel I have much to share.
Through CWF I find expression
And people there who truly care.

I, too, have a gift that I can give;
It is companionship with you.
Sisters in faith, hold firm my hands;
Praise God! Halle-lu, Halle-lu, Halle-lu!


August 8, 1993
Written for CWF study on the Caribbean

## IN SOLIDARITY

In solidarity we weave our baskets,
Strand by strand by strand,
As we learn the meaning of partnership
With a strange and faraway land.
We stand together in the faith.
And praise God's Holy name,
Africans chanting in many languages,
Our worship traditionally the same.

We send our missionaries there,
To teach, to heal, to walk in love,
And through the Holy Spirit
They're blessed by God above.
It's true they suffer hardships,
But, then, they form a bond,
Partners with the ones they serve,
Uplifted by Love's everlasting wand.

I think it is the children
They come to know so well
Who wrap themselves around their hearts,
Writing stories for them to tell.
Children should be the hope of any land;
Children should be the joy of any home.
Children should never be refugees,
Maimed by war, disease and made to roam.

Yes, Africa has its problems,
But, my friends, America has too.
Let's join hands to solve them;
By His Grace He'll see us through.
In solidarity we weave our baskets,
Strand by strand by strand.
As we work for justice, peace, and understanding
Here in America and in that faraway land.

April 28, 1995
Written for CWF study of Africa

55

## POWER AND PROMISE

Lord of Power and Lord of Promise,
We bring our praise to Thee this day.
In every little flower that blooms
Unnoticed by the roadside way,
We catch a glimpse of Heaven's grandeur
And slowly come to understand
How mighty is the grace and power
Of Thy great, omnipotent Hand.

Your Spirit stirs within us
And calls us to obey,
To reach out in love and be a blessing
Like the little flower beside the way.
Lord of Power, Lord of Promise,
We will follow where You lead.
Bless us now and keep us always
Strong in faith, in word and deed. Amen.

June 1, 2002
Written for CWF Program, Power and Promise

## DIGGING WELLS

In the country of Somalia,
Where the land is parched and dry,
Women walk in search of water;
They must find it or they die.

Digging wells can be a lifeline
That we offer them in love;
Knowing that we also bring them
Living Water from above.

Just one well now is our project;
Let our dollars dig it deep.
Let our love flow from it freely,
Provide a harvest we can reap.

In our country of America,
Where we're rich and living's high,
We still search for Living Water;
We must find it—or we die!

Written for 1987 CWF Regional Project to raise $2,340.00,
the cost of digging one well in Somalia. Praise God, we raised the
money, a large portion coming from the sale of my
little book, Digging Wells.

## CWU IN COLUMBIA, SC

I don't know when our unit started
But this is the story I know;
In my twenty-five years of involvement
I've seen it thrive and grow.

Ecumenical we are,
In study, in service and song;
At whatever church we are meeting
You'd think we all did belong.

Women of every faith, race and age
Find joy and satisfaction
In stretching to reach a goal.
This becomes love in action!

Whether it be Day Care,
Meals-on-Wheels or Literacy
We join hands and hearts
To serve Our God above.
Church Women United,
Instruments of His Love!

This poem has been used year after year
in the Church Women United Year Book.

## WHAT ECUMENICAL ACTION IS ALL ABOUT

Ecumenical Action!
It's more than words can say;
It's doing, sharing, serving
In a very special way.

It's making all those health kits
And stuffing brightly colored toys
For migrant workers' children,
Forlorn, bedraggled little girls and boys.

It's sharing food through Harvest Hope
On World Community Day
That many families might survive
In answer to the prayers they pray.

It's sending money for relief
To victims of disaster.
The Red Cross is our channel
And there's no task they can't master.

It's reaching out to this community
And beyond its borders too;
It's saying that we truly care;
In Christ we live and love anew.

We see all people as our brothers;
Indeed the world seems very small.
Praise God! His bounty overflows,
More than enough for all!

So thank you all for helping
In every task we do.
May our heavenly Father look down and bless
The ecumenical action in you.

May 6, 1994
May Fellowship Day, Church Women United

## THE HOMELESS

Have you ever been homeless?
Can you somehow feel the plight
Of those who lost everything
In that hurricane overnight?

I think especially of the children
And the sick and elderly.
How they must miss familiar things
And long to be "home free."

But Moms and Dads must carry on,
Though heavy is their load,
And try to make a loving home
Whatever the abode.

Let's give them some assistance,
And share our blessings true.
But for the Grace of God,
We might be homeless too!


Presented at Church Women United Meeting,
October 10, 1989

## THIS WILL BE A GREAT YEAR

This will be a great year.
Just you wait and see;
Blessings will be showered
From Heaven on you and me!

After the cold of winter
There'll be a life-renewing spring,
Daffodils and crocus
And every growing thing.

Gardeners will be busy sowing.
Hope springs eternal in the heart.
Forgotten are the droughts of summers past;
Dreaming is the winning part!

God's sun will rise each morning,
And as He wills the rains will fall.
Rainbows will span the heavens,
Reminders of His love over all.

God's truth will be the clarion
Of the millennium to come.
His presence will be felt
And His victories won!

Challenges will be met head-on;
Friendships formed and answered prayers.
We'll serve in newness of spirit
As one who understands and cares!

Yes, this will be a great year;
Just you wait and see,
For we'll be constantly looking for the best
So the best is bound to be!

January 1999
Written for Church Women United

## KEEP HOLDING ON

When life seems a struggle;
The sun does not shine;
I'll tell you a secret;
It's His and it's mine:
Keep holding on!

When there are problems,
Oh, too many to count;
You thirst for the water
From His life-giving fount.
Keep holding on!

When you find you can't make it
To the top of life's hill,
Be happy in Jesus
For He's loving you still!
Keep holding on!

Think of the treasures
He bestows on His sheep:
Each day a blessing;
As we sow we shall reap!
Keep holding on!

July 15, 2009

## ABOUT JESUS

When Jesus was a little boy
He lived in a very small town.
All the people knew each other,
But there was no circus clown.

He lived in a flat-roofed house,
Yes, and when the weather was hot
The roof became their sleeping quarters.
The stars looked down and blessed His cot.

He helped Joseph in the carpenter shop;
Indeed he learned the trade.
Wouldn't you just love to see
Something that Jesus had made?

Well you know he grew to be a man,
And he left the little Naz'reth town.
He really didn't have a home;
He roamed the country, up and down.

He made disciples from common people,
Choosing them one by one,
Not for their stature in life
But for what they could become.

The rest of the story is for you and me:
He was crucified for our sins,
But glory to God, he rose from the dead!
His love is alive and always wins!

July 14, 2002
Written for Bible School

## SMILES

Smiles are little messengers
That help us to convey
Loving thoughts to others,
Sometimes, what words can't say.

A boy sees a girl
Across the crowded room.
Timidly, he smiles a greeting,
And love begins to bloom.

A mother on her death bed,
Too ill to say a thing,
Smiles a last farewell,
And slips away on angel-wing.

You cannot count the value of
Those precious little smiles.
I believe that Jesus knew this,
For after trudging many miles

He smiled upon the children,
And said, "Let them come to me."
I bet they smiled right back at Him
As He took them on His knee.

So share your smiles with others,
And smile at Jesus too.
You'll find eternal blessings,
And some made just for you!

August 9, 1990
Written for closing night of Bible School

## THE LORD'S PRAYER

Even as your disciples, longing, came,
Lord, our Lord, we in like manner come today
With that age-old question on our minds.
Master, Teacher, will you teach us to pray?

**"Our Father, who are in Heaven Hallowed be
Thy name."**
Respect Him, obey Him, love Him;
For us the lesson is the same!

**"Thy Kingdom come, Thy will be done
On Earth as it is in Heaven."**
What a wonderful world we'd have
If this truth propelled our thinking,
And caused us to work like leaven.

**"Give us this day our daily bread."**
Not our wishes but our needs He surely
will supply
If in confidence and trust we ask;
On His word we always can rely.

**"Forgive us our trespasses as we forgive those
who trespass against us."**
So easy to say, not so easy to live,
But when we walk encircled in His love
We learn His ways and we forgive.

**"And lead us not into temptation but deliver us
from evil."**
Oh how we need His strength each day
To cast aside the hindrances that beset us
And follow, follow, follow in His way.

Keep us as your children, Lord,
And fill our lives with prayer,
As simple as a little child's
As routinely as breathing air.

Like a flower in its growth reaches upward to the sun
So we grow in spirit as we stretch our souls to Him,
Then in gratitude and praise we come to know
**"Thine is the kingdom and the power and the
glory forever." Amen**

August 1996
Written for Vacation Bible School

## CHECK US OUT

Please feel free to check us out,
Find what our church is all about.
Know we're a family seeking His way,
Needing His strength for each new day;
Praying and praising and dreaming too
Of what, perhaps, we can mean to you;
Listening again as the chimes peal out
Saying for sure what we are about.
Disciples we are with a message to share!
Come let us show how we love and we care!


January 11, 2010
Written for visitor's packet prepared by
Evangelism Committee of
First Christian Church, Columbia, SC.

# FOR EVERY SEASON

For every season
There is a reason
Behind the wonders
God has made.

Now could it be
He made them all for you and me
To enjoy, to appreciate,
To preserve for posterity!

## I PICTURE SPRING

I picture spring
As a child would do,
With a box of crayons
And a challenge new.

I see the expanse
Of a wide, blue sky,
Of grass so green
And violets shy.

I spy a robin
As he hops along,
Looking for food,
Not singing a song.

I hear the bees
At their daily task
Of gathering nectar;
In the tulips they bask.

I picture spring
As a child would do,
And I thank God
For this miracle too!


November 8, 1999
Published in Ideals Magazine Easter 2001

## SPRING

Spring is my favorite season;
I seem to blossom too.
With every yellow daffodil
My strength rebounds anew.

I see God's power spelled out to me
In blossoms pink and white.
Oh, God, I know no one on earth
Could make this lovely sight.

The dogwood has a message
As does the lily too:
The story of the Resurrection;
He died for me and you.

He rose on Easter morning
To be our Redeeming King.
Now we rejoice as we witness Him
In every living thing!

Happy Easter, Happy Spring!

March 9, 2007

## IT'S SPRING IN OUR HEARTS

It's spring in our hearts, dear Father,
When we rise from our buried sin,
And let love with its balm and its healing
Come joyfully rushing in.

It's spring in our hearts, dear Father,
When we yield to Your changes and grow,
When we kneel in Your Garden of Prayer
With seed-thoughts we're needing to sow.

It's spring in our hearts, dear Father,
When the suffering of Jesus we know,
And we feel in our hearts we must follow
The way He directs us to go.

It's spring in our hearts, dear Father,
When we stand with His servants and sing
The rich hallelujahs of Easter,
Crowning Him our Lord and our King!

March 7, 1989

## ARE YOU LISTENING?

Are you listening to the bird-song
When the day is just begun.
Do you hear their joyful music
As you hurry, as you run?

Do you pause to praise your Maker
With our little feathered friends,
And picture in your mind
A peace and calm that never ends?

Are you learning from their lyrics
That their world is ours too;
And what the Bible says about them
Is so right for me and you.

Is it true that they can teach us.
Can it be they understand
God, our Father, has redeemed us,
And He holds us in His Hand.

Then let's join in their singing,
Raise our hearts to Heaven above,
Live our lives forever giving,
Listening for His Voice of Love.


May 26, 1989

## SPRING IN CAROLINA

Spring in Carolina
Is beckoning to me;
Dressed in her prettiest garb
She looks so heavenly.

Azaleas in bright colors
Make up her party dress
While tulips vie with daffodils
To get her sweet caress.

Jessamine forms a crown
To show that she is queen,
And wherever she appears
Her beauty can be seen.

We praise her as the season
When life begins anew.
All living things can testify
That this indeed is true.

Spring in Carolina
Is a treasure rare to see.
It seems our Father smiles upon
This place so dear to me!


November 8, 1999

## SECOND TIME AROUND

They came again this year
And checked the rose vine out.
They flitted here and flitted there,
So happy they could shout.

One day I thought I noticed
The makings of a nest
Just where it was last year.
Why, of course, they know what's best!

They know this is a lovely spot
And perfect as can be;
It's right beside my window,
Convenient for me to see.

Beneath the cool green rose leaves,
Their home was soon complete.
I'd say it was a perfect job,
One no other birds can beat.

We watched Mrs. Cardinal as she laid
And counted eggs, one, two, three;
Then waited for the little birds,
Oh, what a thrill for me.

But soon the thrill was over,
Too soon they fly away.
This was the second time around.
I hope they come another day!

April 1987

## EASTER MORN

Easter morn is different
From any other day;
It rings with hallelujahs
And words that trumpets say!
It beams in all its beauty,
Dewdrops and rising sun,
The backdrop for a hallowed cross
'Round which its message's spun.

Easter comes into our hearts
And opens wide the door
To show us Love personified,
His Grace, our hope and more!
It makes us one in Him above,
His friends, as He did say.
The Christ who died and lives again
Brings joy eternal to every day!

November 8, 1999

## THE EASTER MESSAGE

In the chill and dampness
Of the first Easter morn,
Mary sought her Master,
His body to adorn
With the customary spices
And oils of the day.
This spoke of her great love for Him
In her own humble way.

Amazed to find that someone
Had rolled away the stone,
She stood in awe and wonder,
And frightened to the bone.
An angel spoke in words of comfort,
(He understood her fear.)
"Go, tell to his disciples,
He lives; He is not here."

Mary left the empty tomb
And hastened to obey.
A message of salvation
Was hers to share that day.
Because she loved so deeply,
When needed she was there.
Because she was so faithful,
She was the first to hear.

We, too, should seek the Master
In the early of the morn.
And stand in awe and wonder
'Til in our hearts is born
The message of the resurrection,
Its joy is ever new.
Go tell; the Lord is risen;
He died for me and you!

## AN EASTER SUNRISE SERVICE
## 1943

While it was still yet dark the crowd gathered.
By hundreds we sat on the grassy slope.
Why had so many come?
Were they hungry for answers, strength and hope?

The setting was breathtakingly beautiful.
Strains of Ava Maria wafted the air,
I felt something amazingly special;
I felt that Jesus was there.

His Presence, His Power, His Peace!
With these He fed us that day;
And for a little while we forgot;
World War II seemed eons away!

Then the sun burst forth in its glory.
Trumpets blared as we rose to our feet.
We sang Hallelujah, He is risen!
And God be with you until we meet.

Now I say Happy Easter with a new meaning
And see His face in the people I greet!


March 12, 2007
64 years have passed since I attended this service at
Fort Lincoln Cemetery, Bethesda, Maryland,
but it is still fresh in my memory as Easter comes again in 2007.

## VACATION TIME

The mountain streams and canyons
Are calling out to me.
Vacation time is coming
And here you can be free.
You can forget your trials
And linger for awhile
Beside God's outdoor altar
And see His loving smile!

You can find strength in searching
Some quiet wooded dell
For flowers fair and lovely,
Whose names I cannot tell.
You can kneel down and pluck them
Or leave them growing there;
To witness to God's majesty;
His love is everywhere!

You can pause at noontime
Beside a babbling brook,
And count your many blessings;
Be glad at last you took
The time to see God's beauty,
And feel His loving touch
Upon this land we cherish
And love so very much!

The mountain steams and canyons
Are calling out to me.
They speak in every language;
Come see, come see, come see!
They tell of God's great glory;
They point to Heaven above,
And sing aloud His praises,
His peace and mighty love!

1980

## AN AUTUMN PICTURE

He blends the colors of the leaves
From gold to flaming red;
And makes for us a sight to see;
An autumn flower bed!
From rolling hill to mountain peak,
They glisten in the sun,
And in their quiet beauty
They speak to everyone.

They speak of God who makes us
As different as they are.
With a pattern and a color
And a light to shine afar,
With a purpose to direct us
And a map lest we should stray
From the beaten trail of glory;
The straight and narrow way.

They tell us God can use us
In a lovely autumn scene
When we blend our lives with others,
Peaceful and serene.
His love will lighten up the picture
Like the great and mighty sun,
And be the last amen on earth
When our short days are done.

October 21, 1978
Written on the way to the mountains
for a weekend vacation.

## THE HALLOWEEN PUMPKIN

God took a little pumpkin
From the field in which it grew.
He scrubbed and washed the outside
'Til it looked as good as new.
You know sometimes our outsides
Betray just who we are;
But let's continue with our story
Because its point reaches far.

God took a knife and cut a hole
So He could reach inside.
Then He scooped out all the goop—
Hatred, jealousy, racism,
And things we try to hide.
From the goop He took the seeds;
He washed them and put them out to dry.
These will become new pumpkins,
A generation on which He can rely.

Next He started carving.
Oh, look, He's made a smiling face.
We all know smiles can overcome
And teach us of God's grace.
But, wait, He has not finished.
A lighted candle He places now inside
To tell to all the world
His blessings still abide.

Oh yes, faith, hope and love will always be
The guiding light to victory!

October 23, 2005

## EXPLORERS

In a sense we're all explorers,
Though we do not sail the seas.
We must reckon with adventure,
Let it challenge, let it tease.

We must chart our lives and follow
The one bright star that beckons us,
Like Columbus as he mapped his journey,
'Mid confusion, doubt and fuss.

We must keep our eyes on Jesus,
Let him lead us all the way
To the treasures he has waiting,
To the joys of each new day.

In a sense we're all explorers;
There's a mission for each one.
It's the task at hand that's calling.
Let us work 'til it is done!


Written for Columbus Day, 1987,
when I gave a devotional at
Leisure Time Club, Columbia, SC.

## PISGAH NATIONAL PARK

The rustic mountain living
Of Pisgah beckons me.
The picnic table's waiting,
And there're sights galore to see!

There're trails for all the hikers,
There're streams for those who fish,
There're rivers for canoers;
Just what your heart would wish!

There're places for the campers
To rest when day is done,
Where the smell of hardwood fire
Adds zest to summer fun!

Yes, Pisgah is a Paradise
For young and old alike.
It's God's unspoken love for us,
Whether we swim or fish or bike.

It's a part of His great Plan for us,
So like His gracious giving;
Linger awhile at this beautiful park
And learn about wholesome living!

1980

## THANKSGIVING

Our Pilgrim fathers taught us
The meaning of Thanksgiving,
As they shared their frugal fare
And learned the joys of living.

They thanked God for their blessings,
For life in a wilderness land,
For family and for loved ones,
And the guidance of God's Almighty Hand.

They thanked God for the little things
That meant so much to them,
A rude log cabin, a spring of water,
And homespun garments for Mom to hem.

They thanked God for their freedom,
And this land so new and bold
Was to them a golden treasure
To attain and love and hold.

Yes, our Pilgrim fathers taught us
The meaning of Thanksgiving.
If with our lives we praise the Lord,
We too will know the joys of living.

In faith, in hope, in thanks, our Father,
We seek Thy Holy Face.
Grant us, poor, erring pilgrims,
Your Goodness and Your Grace!

Thanksgiving 1991

## THANKSGIVING

At this happy time of year
Our hearts are filled with love;
We want to fall upon our knees
And thank our God above.

But giving thanks is more than this,
Important as this is;
It's living thanks to verify
That we are truly His.

It's sharing what we have on earth,
And our hope of Heaven too;
It's caring about what's happening
To our world and me and you.

It's rejoicing with God's people
In every big and little thing;
Being whole from the inside out
Will make you shout and sing.

It's harvesting God's blessings,
And counting them once more;
It's saying with a grateful heart,
"I love you, God, like I never have before."

Thanksgiving 1992

## THANKSGIVING, 2002

Thanksgiving is a festive time;
The trees are trimmed in colors bright and gay;
And fields that once were rolling green
Are lined with bales of sun-cured hay.

Thanksgiving is a family time,
A time to travel miles and miles
To share Grandma's traditional feast
Along with chatter, hugs and smiles.

Thanksgiving is a remembering time,
A time when we look back and see
Our Pilgrim fathers come alive
Through pages of our history.
Without their story we would not have
This land so lush and free.
Perhaps today we would not celebrate
America and its liberty.

Thanksgiving is a praising time,
A time to thank our God above
For all the blessings He bestows,
His grace, forgiveness, and His love.

Let us praise the Lord together
On this Thanksgiving Day.

Thanksgiving 2002

## THANKSGIVING THOUGHTS

It's with a truly grateful heart
I bring my thanks to Thee.
Gracious Lord, You've always been
So very good to me.
I look back, a long way back,
To fun-filled youthful days,
Godly parents, impressive mentors
To teach me of Your ways.

When I became your precious child,
Before I was thirteen,
I knew a joy that filled my heart
And reigned with me supreme.
I'm sure I have a guardian angel.
Three times he's saved my life:
Once, before I was yet married,
And twice since becoming a rushed and busy wife.

Your blessings, loving Lord,
Are like the shells of the sea.
We awake to find them every morning,
Just as You promised they would be.
We thank Thee for always walking with us,
Leaving footprints in the sand,
For lighting up the darkest valleys
While holding to our hand.

We know our times are all with You
And the hourglass runs low.
Who but a loving Savior
Waits for us when it's time to go.
It's with a truly grateful heart
I bring my thanks to Thee.
Gracious Lord, You've always been
So very good to me. Amen.

Thanksgiving 2002

## COME, LET US PRAISE THE LORD

Come, let us praise the Lord,
Walk in His heavenly light;
For, as Isaiah prophesied,
He can change our darkest night!

He makes a million stars to shine
And we hear the angels sing
When in humble adoration
Our hearts to Him we bring!

It makes no difference who we are,
Black, or white, Gentile or Jew;
There's room at the lowly manger.
Christ came for me and you!

Come, let us tell the world
A Savior has been born.
His glory shines from His redeemed
Like the sun on a dew-kissed morn!

Come, let us praise the Lord
At this holy Advent time.
Let the love of the little Christ-Child
Permeate your life and mine!

November 1, 2000

## JOURNEY TO BETHLEHEM

As we journey to Bethlehem
We must travel light,
Throw off the trappings
And whatever might
Cause us to miss the joy of this trip.
Watch out, little donkey, lest your feet trip!

We'll meet Mary and Joseph,
That beloved pair,
She, large with child,
Beautiful eyes, long flowing hair;
He, so protective and gentle and kind,
Hides her discomfort, eases her mind!

Slowly we travel up hill and down
Until, weary and worn,
We reach Bethlehem town.
There we encounter the crowds of the day
And the innkeeper who says,
"There's no room to stay;
Find you a stable, a cave, or such;
I'm sorry, indeed, I can't help you much!"

The evening is brief; it fades into night.
The stars are our companions
But there's one so bright
It must be a guardian sent by God, we say,
For Mary now resting on a bed of fresh hay
Awaiting the miracle of Christmas Day!

Without fanfare it happened.
The Christ child was born!
But angels sang out; 'twas a beautiful morn.
There in the stable with the cows and sheep
We bowed to adore Him and watch Him sleep.
And as we touched that sweet baby face
We were filled with His spirit and love and grace.

Now is the journey over
Or has it just begun?
Advent prepares us for a race to be run
And gives us hope for the ages to come!
Thank you, our Father, for sending your Son!

Advent 1998

## COME TO THE TABLE

Come to the table
And find there a place,
Where Jesus is host
And looks in your face!

His love warms out hearts,
His story so true;
He died to redeem us,
To save me and you.

More precious than riches,
Yea, silver and gold,
Is the call to serve Him;
In our hands we hold

The keys to His kingdom
Here on this earth,
To spread His message
And to find our own worth.

Come to the table
And seek out your place.
Jesus will be happy;
He'll smile in your face!

March 9, 2008

## THE HOPE OF ADVENT

The sun is brightly shining;
Old Glory's bravely flying;
But there's terror in our land!
Bombs destroying thousands in the twinkling of an eye;
Anthrax being mailed, an enemy to defy!
What evil-doers will do next
No one can foretell.
What we do know they have taught us:
This war, this 21st century War, is Hell!

In a similar setting
Our Savior came to earth.
Angels from the realms of glory announced that Holy Birth.
He came to save us from our sins,
To bring us Peace and Joy!
Oh, what a task was his to do, that precious baby boy!
He did not bring a sword or spear;
He was only armed with love.
That love has lived 2000 years
And draws us to our home above!

As we come again to Advent
Let's prepare our hearts anew,
To worship at the lowly manger,
And bring our treasures too.
Let's thank God that bombs can't stop us,
And Satan will not have his way!
We'll stand! We'll sing!
We'll praise our God forever
For Hope that was born on that first Christmas Day!

December 2001

## JESUS CHRIST WAS BORN

In a simple, lowly place
Jesus Christ was born,
While the world esteemed Him not,
And many of His own.

But angels sang His Message
On that night so soft and still,
And filled the skies with praises
Of peace and joy, goodwill.

Mary gently nurtured Him
As Joseph watched aghast,
A wee bundle of humanity,
Their Savior come at last.

Their Savior is our Savior,
The Savior of the earth.
And that's the joy of Christmas;
To all He gives new birth.

We see Him in each thing we do.
We feel His presence near,
It is His Love we share with you
Throughout each passing year!

Merry, Merry Christmas.


December 1988

## WARM HOLIDAY WISHES
## FROM
## THE STEVENS

Christmas is remembering dear ones like you.
Thank God for the mem'ries and miracles too!

Christmas is preparing for family,
From roasting the turkey to trimming the tree;
Baking the cookies and pound cakes galore;
Wrapping the gifts and shopping some more;
Hanging the stockings on Christmas Eve night,
Feeling the warmth from the fireside bright.

Christmas is finding true joy in sharing,
Letting His little ones know we are caring.

Christmas is worshipping at the manger bed,
Feeling afresh by His Spirit led,
Kneeling to touch His baby face,
Receiving forgiveness, love and grace.

May God richly bless you we humbly pray
As we celebrate the meaning of Christmas Day!

Our love and prayers,
Caroline and Pappy

Christmas Cards, 2002

## CHRISTMAS IS LOVE

Christmas is Love.
How do I know?
I go to the Bible
And it tells me so.

I turn to the page
John 3:16.
The words are so simple;
Children know what they mean.
God so loved the world
That He gave us His Son.
Anyone who believes
(Praise the Lord, anyone)
Can have life eternal
And joy in his heart,
Of the family of God
Become a real part!

Yes, this is the message
From Heaven above.
Christmas is giving
And Christmas is Love!

Christmas is Love.
You ask how I know.
I see it in faces
That radiantly glow;
In the old and the young
And the little ones too;
As they pause for a moment
From things that they do
To sing as with angels
On that beautiful morn.

Glory to God;
A Savior is born!

Yes, this is the message
From Heaven above.
Christmas is singing
And Christmas is Love!

Christmas is Love.
How do I know?
I turn back the pages to a night long ago
When men knelt and worshipped
At a crude manger bed;
And knew in their hearts
That God was not dead!
He was there in the stable
And He's here in this place.
And each time we seek Him
We learn of His Grace!

Yes, this is the message
From Heaven above!
Christmas is worship
And Christmas is Love!

## IT'S CHRISTMAS

When my house if filled with gladness
And the hearth is all aglow,
The gifts are wrapped and waiting
And there's talk of mistletoe,
Then I feel the Yuletide Spirit
And what joy it brings my heart
As I see the Christ Child lifted
In each precious little part
Of preparing for His Birthday,
Of remembering He's a King,
And of placing adoration
On this sweet and simple thing!

When the candles bright are burning
And they hold a meaning true,
Then within each heart is yearning
This one Christmas wish for you.
May the treasures of this Season,
With their love and sparkling cheer,
Ever guide and lead you onward
To a bright and happy year.
May the things we hold in common
Ever bind us in His Will
And the roads that we may travel
Beckon to a shining hill!

1980

## CHRISTMAS IS OUR CORNERSTONE

Christmas is the cornerstone
That holds our family.
We clasp our hands in gratitude
And raise our hearts to Thee.

Now bless us, our Father,
Forgive our foolish ways.
Please guide our steps aright
And keep us all our days.

Accept our humble thanks
For every Christmas gift.
You've been so good to us,
Our searching souls you lift.

You lead us on our journey,
We never need to walk alone.
You are the light of Christmas
And Christmas is our cornerstone.

Christmas 1984

## ESPECIALLY AT CHRISTMAS

Especially at Christmas
There's a journey we must make.
The urge is most compelling,
But wait; which road shall we take?

Like the wise men of the Bible
We start just where we are,
And looking to the heavens
We find that special star.

Our faith will help us follow
When disappointments come;
For are we not out searching
For that precious, Holy One?

When at last the journey's over,
And we worship at His feet,
Our hearts are filled with joy;
We feel somehow complete.

But then a Voice tells us,
As it did to those three Kings,
Rise up! Return another way
To make known these wondrous things;

To share the love of Christmas,
To behold the glorious Star,
To know He is our Savior!
Thank you, Jesus, for who You are!

1999

## I THINK YOU CALL IT GREED

It's organized confusion,
But it's a lot of fun.
It holds each one's attention
Until the game is done.

Manipulation is the word
And, yes, a deal or two.
Who knows where this gift will go;
Or if I'll get it back from you.

Excitement girds the circle
As we draw and lose and win.
Oh, it's just a Christmas sport,
But it speaks to me of sin.

I see the world in retrospect
And as it is today,
A game of wheeling, dealing,
And "Oh, I want my way."

The secret is to play the game
And not adopt its creed.
I don't know its rightful name,
But I think you call it GREED.

December 11, 1988
We played this game at our Sunday School party at
Doug and Ginny Schmoltze's home.
There were 35 of us in the circle and we had a barrel of fun.
Charles McLean suggested I write a poem about it
so I gave it a shot.

## THIS NEW YEAR

Thank you, our Father,
For giving us this year.
We pray we'll use it wisely
For the fleeting years are dear.

We look back and remember
The good times and the bad.
Always we will treasure
The great fellowship we've had.

We look now to the future,
Expectant as can be
That you will lead us onward,
For we place our trust in Thee.

We come now as your children,
Each with a task to do.
Please help us in the doing
And we'll give the praise to you.

Use us in your service
Is what we humbly pray,
And keep us looking upward
Our hands in yours each day!

January 1, 1989

## VALENTINE'S DAY

Valentines are fragile things,
Fashioned of paper, bows and lace,
But they speak of something very strong,
The bond of friendship, love and grace.

We go to the Bible and there we learn
What friendship was meant to be.
David and Jonathan, Ruth and Naomi;
Just think of the impact of their lives
And how they shaped history.

Now speaking of love, remember Jacob,
How he met Rachel at the well,
Loving her at first sight.
Fourteen years he'd wait for her,
Working for her father from morn till night.

The story of Ruth and Boaz
Is a beautiful love story, too.
In a different day and a different age,
But God's hand was writing upon each page.
And down through the years it came to be
That Jesus was born of this family tree.

Jesus, we know, is the epitome
Of friendship and love and yes, God's grace.
The red heart of the Valentine
Reminds us that He
Gave all that He had; His life, His blood,
To purchase salvation for you and me.

When we stand at the cross,
Or we kneel down to pray,
Let's thank God for our Savior.
Happy Valentine's Day!

January 30, 1999

# SPECIAL EVENTS AND SPECIAL PEOPLE

There are so many special events
Which now are history.
I'm grateful to have been a part of them,
Precious gems of memory.

There are special people also
Who have touched my life
In one way or another.
Lord, bless them all, I pray.
In Christ, they are my sister and my brother!

## OUR NATION'S BIRTHDAY

With humble thanks to God
We raise Old Glory high
And celebrate our nation's birthday
On this another Fourth of July!
We feel a new sense of responsibility
To those who lived and loved and died
For the freedom of America,
Where we are privileged to abide.

We recall today some of those
Who made the pages of her history,
Nathan Hale, Paul Revere, George Washington,
Thomas Jefferson, Benjamin Franklin, Patrick Henry.
These were counted as the greats,
But equally as important to me,
Are those who lie in Flanders Field
And the unmarked graves of the Confederacy.

I think of that lonely Italian immigrant
Who found refuge in this land
And painted the figures around the rotunda
Of our nation's capitol building.
A Michelangelo without a stirring band.
For twenty-five years he labored
Often from a scaffold, lying on his back.
The floor one hundred eighty feet below.
Devotion, perseverance and courage he certainly did not lack.
One night he died in his sleep,
Leaving his great memorial behind.
Today an American flag flies over his grave,
Honored by Congress, he was one of a kind.

Upon his death it was discovered
He gave almost all of his earnings away
To our needy and underprivileged
As an expression of his gratitude
For freedom and peace
And the right to tearfully say,
"I am an American citizen;
God bless this land today!"

God keep this land forever
A true democracy
With a mission to make
And share the peace;
So others like the artist Brumidi
May find their dreams and sweet release.
We salute and honor those in uniform,
Especially the brave and brilliant warriors of our day.
Together let us all serve America
As God directs our thinking and our way!

July 4, 1999

## MY MOTHER TOLD ME

My Mama told me life is what you make it;
It can be like a song
If we know whose we are
And to whom we each belong!

My Mama told me to never shirk my duty,
Look heavenward, dream and pray,
Brighten my own little corner,
Praise God for each new day!

My Mama told me to hold my head up high,
And on that plane to ever live,
Humbly seeking and serving Him
Who beckons us to our home up in the sky.

When I was little, my Mama told me
To always wash behind my ears.
Now as I bathe, I remember her
With smiles and love and tears.

My Mama told me to give to the world the best you have
And the best will come back to you.
I've lived long enough to know
These words are sweet and oh, so true!

Written for Mother-Daughter Banquet 2002

## A LAST SALUTE TO THE 355TH ENGINEER REGIMENT

Here's to a grand old Regiment
As it fades into history,
Leaving mem'ries which have become treasures
For people like you and me.
Yes, you were the greatest generation;
You gave no less than your best
To God and country and family,
Building bridges which have stood time's test!

You were young and brave and daring;
Determined that America should win,
To bring peace and honor and stability
To all the world again,
Of course, it was a bitter battle
To bring old Hitler down
And many, many lives were lost
From countryside and town!

But how we cheered and thanked our God
When you came marching home,
And we who kept the home fires burning
Knew vict'ry's sweetest joy: to never, ever be alone.
Now life would be so different;
Life would start anew,
And, by God's grace and with His help,
We'd make our dreams come true!

In the many years that's passed since then
We've met for "old time's" sake;
We shared our stories, wiped our tears,
And vowed that we would make
One more Reunion lest we forget
That bridge across the Rhine,
The symbol of the 355th,
Which binds your hearts and mine!

Although this is the last Reunion
I'm sure we'll keep in touch,
For friendship is a lasting thing;
To each it means so much.
Now as we salute a grand old Regiment
We pause for this parting prayer:
God grant to us a special blessing
And keep us always in Thy care!

Written by request for the last Reunion of
355th Engineer Regiment
Held at Perrysburg, Ohio, September 24-27, 2000.

## THE OLD CHURCH AND THE NEW

They stand beside the highway,
The old church and the new,
One brimming full of history;
The other holding a challenge for me and you.

One speaks of all the dear souls
Who came to worship here;
Of good times and of bad times
And how we learned to care.
For one brief moment, I pause to recollect
My childhood in this church;
Sunday School beneath a tree
And picnics we loved so much.

The old pump organ, wood-burning stove,
Communion at the altar rail;
Special programs for Children's Day,
And lest my memory fail
The preaching and the singing
Made Sunday a hallowed day,
And the treasure of my heart, it seems,
Was to hear my mother pray.

The new church speaks of growth,
Three choirs singing praise,
And many happy little cherubs
To blossom in future days.
There are old familiar faces
And some I do not know,
But in God's kingdom we all are one;
His love has made it so.

I see that love in every gift
Bestowed to this great church.
I'm sure the givers all were blessed
Because they loved so much.
The cross hangs there to testify
To a love that's greater still;
It beckons us to follow Him,
Our lives with purpose fill.

Beulah United Methodist Church,
You've come a long, long way.
Over 100 years you've been serving;
We truly honor you this day;
And pray God's richest blessings
On each member of your congregation.
You've shown what a community can do
When they work together in a Christ-like relation.

They stand beside the highway,
The old church and the new;
One fading into history,
The other holding a challenge for me and you!


November 17, 1998
Written after having attended the dedication
Of Beulah's new chapel, Sandy Run Community of
Calhoun County.

## HOMECOMING

Homecoming.....Coming home!
It means the same to me.
People greeting people
Like a loving family.

It's fun and food and fellowship.
It's mem'ries brought to light
Of the greatness of this Church,
And a hope for her future bright.

Homecoming....Coming home!
Oh, what a happy time,
A time to count the blessings
That fill your lives and mine.

A time to sing God's anthems,
A time to bow and pray,
To sup with one beside you.
Let love be shared today.

Let goals be set within our hearts.
Let Jesus have His way.
Together let us praise the Lord
On this Homecoming Day!

June 5, 1988

## HOMECOMING

On days like this when we assemble,
And call back times now past,
We feel a blessed warmth of spirit;
It binds and holds us fast.
We lift our hearts in gratitude
To our Father, Lord and King,
And with our whole beings
Our praise to Him we sing!

How good it is to be a part
Of this beloved church,
Where we have learned and served
And grown so very much.
It's really like a second home
To many here today;
Its beacon light is always shining
To guide us on life's way!

So welcome home to First Christian;
Welcome home to celebrate.
Let's make this an annual occasion,
Yes, a day to commemorate;
A day to feast and fellowship
At God's table waiting here,
Remembering departed loved ones
And what to them was dear.

A day to ponder and consider
What our mission truly is,
And to rededicate our lives
To God and what is His.
So bless us now, Our Father,
As we go our several ways;
Help us to keep the faith
And live for Christ always.
Amen.

August 24, 1997

## HOMECOMING

First Christian greets you warmly
On this very special day.
Her children scattered widely
Are coming home to pray,
Coming home to worship,
Coming home to sing,
Coming home to celebrate
The joy our blessings bring!

We have pastors, teachers, pupils,
Retirees and those who're going strong,
But we're bonded in one fellowship
And we sing the same sweet song:
Praise God from whom all blessings flow,
Amazing Grace, how sweet the sound,
And Jesus loves me this I know!

Yes, His spirit is among us;
I see it in each smiling face
As we greet and reminisce
And thank God for His grace.
Let's eat and drink to His glory,
Commemorate this homecoming day.
You've come home because you love us
And we love you the selfsame way!

August 23, 1998

## HOMECOMING

Homecoming! What a happy thought!
Friends greeting friends in the good old fashioned way.
As, yes, I see families reuniting,
And I'm sure this is going to be a lovely day!

Let this joy last forever, Lord, we pray.

Homecoming! What a blessed thought!
It conjures up mem'ries only we would understand;
The funny times, the sunny times,
And the sad times when we held each other's hand.

Lord, keep us remembering.

Homecoming! What a sacred thought!
Think of all the homecomings in the Biblical age.
Agape love, forgiveness, gratitude, humility;
They're all between the lines on page after page.

Lord, bless us as we reach up to Thee.

Homecoming! What a glorious thought!
A time together here on earth, you and I,
But then a call, and we are gone
To sing our hallelujahs up there in the sky.

Lord, for now and always, we praise Thy Holy Name.
Amen.

October 3, 2004

## HAPPY BIRTHDAY, LIBBY KERCHUSKY

Here's to a lady who celebrates life;
Just follow her if you dare.
To our DWF she's a treasure;
We think she's a jewel rare!

It's family that matters to Libby;
It's church and friends and such.
It's being there when needed;
Little things means so much!

But it's not all work with Libby.
Somehow there's always time for fun;
The golf course is inviting,
Who says her swinging days are done?

On your special day we salute you,
For you are our shining star!
Ninety years young and still growing;
We love you just as you are!

Happy Birthday, Libby!


December 1, 2007

## TO AGAPE CHRISTIAN CHURCH

Through agape love this church was built
To glorify God's name.
When His Spirit filled this congregation,
Setting your hearts aflame,
You worked as one till the job was done,
And victory you could claim!

Through agape love this structure stands,
Calling us all to obey,
It offers a message for the new millennium:
Hope for the future; strength for the day,
And God's guiding hand each step of the way!

Through agape love this church reaches out,
Its mission is the world.
To the young and the old
And especially those who have never heard.
Its story will be told continually:
Our God is a mighty God;
Our God is a majestic God;
Our God loves you and me!

In the tone of such love we gather here
On this blessed day of dedication
Praising God together
And rejoicing with you
In this your deserved celebration.
Sister churches in Christ we are,
Writing our pages of history.
Yours is a special one to remember;
You rightly bear the name Agape!

June 27, 1999
Written for the dedication of
Agape Christian Church's new church building.

## BACK TO WASHINGTON

I'm off to a Washington tea party,
And I am a belle of the ball.
In lace I'll appear, society to fear,
For I feel I'm the least of all.

Once a telegram came to my home
When I felt I was still a young girl.
It called me to come to the capital,
And my days then became a big swirl.

A career and a romance were waiting,
And I was to start a new life,
Working long hours for the government
While fulfilling my role as a wife.

Now a poetrygram arrives in the mail.
It beckons me back to the place
Where mem'ries abound as the statues,
And I only remember one face.

A poem has made the difference;
Some words I just wrote from my heart.
I am told I'll receive an award,
But aren't mem'ries the greatest part?

I'm off to a Washington tea party.
Now it's back to a different D.C.
The award I find there cannot compare
To the love that once waited for me!

June 27, 1989
Written after receiving a poetrygram to come to Washington, D.C.
to receive the golden poet's award offered by Poetry World
at their 5th Convention being held over Labor Day weekend 1989,
at the Washington Hilton Hotel.

## ONE HUNDRED YEARS OF COVENANT

For one hundred years of covenant
We'll remember 1992.
Let's congregate; let's celebrate
And make our pledge anew.

Women of the Christian Church,
Look back across the years,
And take a bow for where we are;
Rejoice and shed some tears.

Some gave their lives in service
Far from their own loved land;
Some scaled the heights of leadership
From the touch of Jesus' hand.

Some worked in local churches,
No sunshine in which to bask;
They pitched right in and did the job,
Dedicated to their task.

But Jesus knew and blessed them;
He's brought us to this day,
Women in covenant with God,
Women who love and work and pray.

For one hundred years of covenant
We'll remember 1992.
Let's congregate; let's celebrate.
And make our pledge anew!

Written for 1992 CWF Regional Retreat,
Celebrating 100 years of women's work,
from Missionary Society to Christian Women's
Fellowship of today.

## A TWENTY-FIFTH BIRTHDAY

A special lady has a birthday
And she is twenty-five years old.
Churches will celebrate;
They will commemorate
As the pages of her life unfold.

She is an interesting person,
Enchanting and loving and kind.
She is white; she is black;
And sometimes she is brown.
But she's so beautiful in soul and mind.

She invites you to her party
And to stay a long, long while
To work with her,
To pray with her,
And catch that winning smile.

She's no stranger to us
For she's akin to you and me.
Come let's cheer her,
Our World CWF,
On her 25th Anniversary!

September 1980

## HOPE FOR THE JOURNEY

From every state and overseas
They found a meeting place,
Christian women of our church,
No matter their age or race.

What brought them on this journey?
What treasure did they find?
Was it worth four years of waiting;
Is this "hope" just a state of mind?

The answers they found are many
And there're many that will last
When the mem'ries of Purdue have faded,
And the years have swiftly passed.

We're happy for South Carolina;
We stood proudly with the rest,
Wearing our hats with State emblem,
While praising the Name we love best.

Some of our ladies were ushers;
Some were stewards and convenors too;
Some were dining room hostesses,
One a deacon and one an enabler true.

To each we say, "Thank you for serving,"
But I'm sure you would do it again,
Just to be a part of that gathering,
And to hear the church say, "AMEN."

Almost 5000 ladies attended
And each has her story to tell
Of the 7th Quadrennial Assembly,
'Twas a journey to a soul-quenching well!

June 29, 1982
Written for 7th International Christian Women Fellowship
Quadrennial Assembly, held at Purdue University,
West Lafayette, Indiana.

## A DREAM COME TRUE

She was a pretty young teacher with a dream or two,
Seeking a kindergarten but what could she do?
At that time Columbia had exactly none.
To solve the problem she'd have to start one!

She shared her dream with her husband one day:
We'll add a room onto our house;
It'll have to be big. Now what do you say?
Hesitant at first, but, of course it was done.
Soon the patter of little feet as they came one by one
Brought assurance to them with each new morn
'Twas the right thing to do; Timmerman School was born!

Soon the room was overflowing
With bright, shining faces
Eager to learn from a teacher
Who could take them places.
Like the fairytale woman
Who lived in a shoe
June had so many children
She didn't know what to do.

Several rentals they secured served for awhile
But ultimately she knew,
With a wink and a smile,
The time had come!
They must build a real school;
One with high standards would be their rule.

Now fifty years later
We stand and we cheer
As laurels are presented
To this teacher so dear,
Who followed her dream
Until it came true.
God bless you, June Timmerman!
We all love you!


November 2005
Happy 50th Anniversary to a top notch school
and to all who helped to make it so!

## TO PAULINE MCKIBBEN

What a milestone you have met!
Ah, what a mystery
To outlive oh so many friends,
A page for history!

We think of all you have accomplished!
We love you for the doing,
An example for us to follow
And find joy in pursuing.

God bless you on your birthday,
This very special one!
God keep you all your days;
Fill them with joy and fun.

Happy 100th Birthday!


January 22, 2008

## DEDICATION OF HANDBELLS IN MEMORY OF
## SUZANNE ARRINGTON

All too soon she left us;
All too soon she slipped away
To a land where there's always music,
And His angels celebrate day after day.
Yes, I think they dance and sing for joy
Around the heavenly throne
As they welcome home God's children,
Claimed by Jesus as His own!

Suzanne was one who shared His love
Until she could no more;
And now that love rings out today
Expressed more sweetly than before.
As we listen to these handbells
Given in her memory
Let's truly listen with our hearts,
For their message speaks to you and me.

The message is reach out in love
And help someone to live.
Be thankful for each day you have;
Wake up, cheer up, and please forgive!
Life is too short upon this earth
To let old Satan get us down.
Just walk with Christ; He'll hold our hands
And lead us to that bright celestial town!

These bells won't ring without the ringers,
A sacred task; or did you know?
Remember that we are Christ's body,
His hands, His feet, His voice soft and low.
The story must be told; it's ours to tell today;
So ring the bells, the bells within your heart
And celebrate this precious gift of music.
Suzanne, your love lives on; from it we'll never part!

December 7, 1997

## ABOUT BARBARA ENTWISTLE

The questions have been answered
In a clear and concise way,
But there lingers in my mind
Something I needs must say.
Barbara is deserving,
Deserving of the best,
For that is what she gives.
She stands out from the rest.

With her talents and abilities
She commands a leader's role,
And whatever task she's doing
You can know she'll reach her goal.
Filled with enthusiasm
And a willingness to work,
She becomes an example
To anyone who would shirk.

She's a worker in God's vineyard;
That's plain for all to see,
But, best of all, she's a friend,
A friend to you and me.
She makes the way seem simple;
She walks it every day;
And many times together
We bow our heads and pray.

We're reaching out together
In compassion and in love,
Seeking to be used
By our Father up above.
And Barbara is our leader
Yes, she's our shining star.
Let's make her "Disciple of the Year,"
For, Barbara, that's what you really are!

September 1997

126

## TO TORRIE AND CHRISTY

You came to us when we were much in need
Of what you had to give,
Of pastoring and shepherding
And teaching us how to live.

Although we called you from a larger church,
A place that you called home,
We rejoice in the choice you made,
To cast your lot with us and never roam.

Now, Torrie, you're writing your name in S.C.
Again and again you're called upon to lead,
Making us proud of First Christian, Columbia,
Upholding our standing in word and deed.

It seems the move was good for Christy also.
Ah, yes, she's found her niche at last:
Teaching in the medical field;
A challenge, but, oh, what a blast!

We wish you both God's blessings
As together we serve Jesus each day,
Looking to Him, our Leader of Leaders,
Knowing He's truly the Light of our way!

January 12, 2007
Written for our present pastor, Rev. F. Torrance Osgood,
and his lovely wife, Christy Beach.

## GREATER THINGS

"Ye have not chosen me,
But I have chosen you,
And ordained you,
That ye should go and bring forth fruit."
Thus spoke our Master to His disciples
As he installed them in their roles
Of witnessing and testifying,
Of reaching out in love and saving souls!

So on this day of installation,
Steve and Donna,
Jesus speaks the same to me and you,
And adds a postscript, if you please,
"Greater things than these you will do."
What are the greater things, Lord?
And where do we go from here?
Just hold on to the Master's hand
And He will take you there!

Out there on the horizon
Looms a dream for this great church,
And you've been sent to lead us;
Already we love you very much.
Together we will seek and serve our God.
Together we will pray.
Together we will find those greater things.
God bless you on this Installation Day!

Written for Installation Service for Steve and
Donna Doan, pastors of First Christian Church,
Columbia, SC, August 2, 1998.

## A TRIBUTE TO JUDY DUDLEY

Madam President, the meeting is now called to order
And our purpose is to say
Your cabinet is indeed very sorry
That you are going away.

The minutes reveal how you've led us
In the short time you've been here.
Your can-do spirit is contagious
And has helped us to have a great year!

There's no old business we can think of,
Only praise for what has been done.
Our giving is at a high level;
What was work has now become fun!

We'll miss you as you leave us
To answer the Master's call;
But our love and our prayers go with you.
Shalom, dear Judy, Shalom from us all!


July 24, 1999
Written for Judy Dudley, Regional CWF President.
Her husband, Rev Dudley was being called to another
church. I was Judy's secretary.

## TO JOHN AND LORETTA CAPIZZI

In this modern age of broken relationships,
divorces and such,
How refreshing it is to celebrate
a 50th Wedding Anniversary
With a couple we've come
to love so much!

John and Loretta, we did not know you
when you were wed.
But we can imagine that beautiful
moment in your lives
When, by flickering candlelight,
your vows were said.

New Yorkers you were,
Californians, too;
But now in Columbia you've planted your feet,
Contributing much to the life of our church,
Forming bonds of friendship lasting and true.

This evening we join in your celebration,
Crowning you with our love,
And praying God's blessings upon you.
May He write your names on a golden page;
For your marriage is a testament to this day and age!

Happy Fiftieth Wedding Anniversary

November 6, 2004

## TO JEANNE AND ED WILLIAMS

On this, your wedding day
We join in wishing you
A journey filled with happiness
And a love that's fresh and new.

May each day be an adventure
In your land of "dreams come true."
May the beauty of your life together
Be like a rainbow encircling you.

May your faith in God direct you
As you look to Him and pray,
And feel His presence with you
With the coming of each day.

God bless you, Jeanne and Ed!
We love you,
Happy, Happy Wedding Day!


February 2005

## THEY HAVE BLESSSED MY LIFE

I don't know what good I've done;
Only God knows that,
But I know they've blessed my life
In fleeting moments when I sat
And chatted cheerfully,
Shared a gift, a poem, a prayer,
Touched them with love;
Reached out to say I care.

These names were not assigned to me,
But rather I was drawn to everyone:
Ruth Wright, blind and crippled,
Lonely but witty, wise and lots of fun;
Delia Roof, a neighbor, bedridden,
Oh, for many years;
To know her was to love her
And to feel her pain and fears.

Caroline Green was someone special,
A member of my CWF Group;
She saved news articles for me to read;
Yes, we shared more than chicken soup.
Sarah Smith, oh, how I miss her still;
To me and Pappy she was a dear, dear friend.
Crippled with arthritis, she lived so gallantly,
Fighting the disease which had its way
And conquered in the end.

There have been many others,
Not to mention family.
Somehow it seems the blessing
Has returned full-fold to me
Whenever I have taken time
To serve God in this way.
I always know that He'll be with me,
And He has been every day.


April 6, 1997
Written for Elders' Prayer Breakfast when we
gave reports on our visitation in conjunction with
our study on Christian Caregiving.

## TEACHERS

I've had a lot of teachers
And I've been a teacher too.
Teachers are like preachers;
They share their lives with you!

It's not just book material
We impart to listening ears;
It's how we live each passing day
And share our joys and tears.

We represent the Christ
When we extend a helping hand.
We find ourselves in living
And know that life is grand!

Of all the teachers I have had
There's one that stands apart;
It's not just the words he says;
It's what we feel is in his heart.

Louie Crouch, we love you!
With one voice we want to say,
Thank you from your Christian Crusaders;
Have a blessed Christmas Day!

December 12, 2008

## TO OUR SENIOR CITIZENS

This little church has a message,
A story it knows so well.
And, if it could speak, dear people,
These are the things it might tell.

You've gathered today to honor
Those whom you love and adore.
You call them senior citizens,
But to me they are really much more.

They are the heart of this building;
They fill its portals with praise.
Down this aisle they have walked in their gladness,
Wearing happiness for all of their days.

Down this aisle they have brought their loved ones
And wept as they laid them to rest,
Leaving all to the ways of the Master
Believing He cares and knows best.

They've given themselves in service.
They've shared and toiled and dreamed.
They've inspired their children to climb,
Reaching higher than they, it has seemed.

But our Father in Heaven who judges
And rewards us for what has been done
Will bless these dear senior citizens
And make of them saints one by one.

1973
Written for Seniors' Day at Beulah United Methodist Church,
Sandy Run, SC (my childhood church).

## THE WINDOW AT THE HOSPITAL

The window at the hospital
Reveals two worlds to me,
The sick, the sad, the suffering
And the hustling, bustling free.

On one side are the nurses
Attending each ill one,
Implementing orders,
Seeing each task is done.

On the other is construction,
With derrick and pulley in place,
Men spreading fresh concrete
While ambulances continue their race.

People look small from the window,
And cars like a modern-day game;
They all fit together somehow,
For life goes on just the same.

How small we must look
From God's window,
He sees both sides of the pane;
He gives all our manifold blessings,
Sending the sunshine and rain.

September 15, 1989

## THANK YOU, LORD, FOR FATHERS

Thank you, Lord, for fathers
Who stand so straight and tall,
And never let their burdens
Weigh them down at all.

Thank you, Lord, for fathers
Who give and love and pray
That we might know the blessings
Of a new and better day.

Thank you, Lord, for fathers
Who somehow find the time
To do the little things
Near to your heart and mine.

Memories to cherish
When the birds have flown the nest;
When days turn into years,
And Dads are laid to rest.

Thank you, Lord, for fathers,
The young and growing-old,
The shadows that they cast
On a world that's growing-cold.

We thank you, Lord, for families
And hearths at night that glow
Around that central figure,
The dear old Dad we know.


With my own departed Dad as a model,
I wrote this poem for a friend,
to use at her church on Father's Day, 1979.

137

## A FATHER'S DAY TRIBUTE

Today we pay a special tribute
To the fathers of our time;
For in one way or another
They've touched your lives and mine.
Our children walk in their footsteps,
Surer of the paths they'll tread
Because a father strong in character
Made an imprint easily read.

By example they have shown us
What is virtue and goodwill,
How these bring joy to mundane living
And blessings our lives to fill.
Warriors of wars and keepers of the peace,
They take a stand on what they think is right
At home, at church, and in the workplace, too,
Torchbearers who gladly share their light.

The light they share is an eternal one;
It comes down from our Father up above.
It's been passed from one generation to another,
And sometimes we have even called it love.
It holds our homes together
And makes our churches grow;
It's the only thing in all the world
Worth dying for, we know.

Today we pay a special tribute
To the fathers of our day.
Close to our hearts we hold you;
God bless you all, we pray.

Father's Day 1999

138

## THANK YOU, "SMITTY"

He scrubs and shines and chases dirt
All over this big church;
The gleaming floors will testify
That someone loves them very much!

Yes, "Smitty" cares that things are right,
In ship-shape order, if you please.
He's always ready for inspection
And he does it with the greatest ease.

He feels the tug of responsibility,
The joy of a job well done.
Our hats are off to you, "Smitty!"
Yes, I think our hearts you've won!

Thank you for being our very best custodian!


September 6, 1998

## A TRIBUTE TO MOTHER

Of all the days we celebrate
For one reason or another,
One stands apart, within our hearts,
This day, when we honor Mother.

Now whether she's Mother or "Mama"
She deserves our laurels and praise,
For the treasures of a lifetime
Are the mem'ries of her loving ways.

My own dear Mother was "Mama."
Oh, how she blessed that name!
She brought to it gentleness and beauty,
Not riches or fortune or fame.

She left me a challenge to follow
And to pass on to my children too.
Dear God, I pray for the courage
To live by her standards true.

I pray that the old-fashioned values
Will live on through the eons of time
As a tribute to all noble mothers,
Whose lives are like lyrics sublime!

Presented at church on Mother's Day,
May 14, 1989

## CHRISTIAN MOTHERS

Christian mothers are like flowers.
They lift their souls to God above,
And He causes them to blossom
Through the sunshine of His love.

Christian mothers are like flowers.
They just brighten up the way,
For through their wisdom come the answers
To many problems of our day.

Christian mothers are like flowers
With nurture they multiply,
And give back to God who gave them
Countless blessings before they die.

Christian mothers are like flowers.
We know we'll see them again,
For they teach us His promise is sure,
Like the gentle promise of His rain.

Christian mothers deserve their flowers.
Yes, they've earned them every one,
Though they'll be the last to admit it,
Let's thank them for what they have done!

Mother's Day 1990

## MY ROCKING CHAIR REVERIE

In the quiet of the evening,
'Round the Christmount fireplace,
We sat in rocking chairs
To seek our Savior's grace.

We had seen Him in His grandeur
Of mountain peaks and streams;
We had beheld Him in the beauty
Of leaves and sun-light gleams.

We had felt His love among us
As we laughed and had great fun;
We had shared a fellowship
That's not known to everyone.

We had learned about each other,
And a bit of history,
But the words I read in stone
Do not say as much to me

As the warm and gracious welcome
Of two friends of yesterday.
They are etched within my heart
And I'm sure they'll always stay.

These reflections mark our journey
As I close my reverie.
Please bless us all, dear Father,
And keep us close to Thee.

Written after Leisure Time Club trip to mountains of
North Carolina, including overnight stay at Christmount
and visit to Neal and Sarah Wyndham, October 28-29, 1992.

## OUR ACOLYTES

Today we honor our acolytes,
For to them real praise is due.
Faithful they've been in their service,
Lending reverence and dignity too.

Whether we're ministers or acolytes
God sees us and loves us the same,
For the thing most important to Him
Is that we glorify His Name.

It's not just a candle you're lighting;
It's a message that you must convey:
Our God is the LIGHT of the world.
Please take it to someone today!


April 1, 1990

## REMEMBERING BILLY BELLINGER

We were in first grade together
Eighty-some years ago
In a little country schoolhouse,
Where there was learning,
And time was slow.

Our teacher was a spiritual leader,
Who early planted seeds;
She saw in us potential
And tried to meet our needs.
Upon such a firm foundation
Billy was bound to grow
Into the wonderful person he became;
Beloved and blessed and a joy to know.

He rose to the heights of his profession,
But in his humble way
He was just a caring family man
Who looked forward to the day
When he could return to Sandy Run
To relive those times of old;
To relax, to dream, and remember
Meant more to him than gold.

Nancy and children and sister "Toug,"
Cherish your mem'ries each day;
Look through your tears to our Father above
And know He is leading the way.
As we celebrate Billy's life
We feel he is witnessing too,
Peeking down with the angels from Heaven
Saying, "Come, I am waiting for you!"

February 17, 2007

## A MEMORIAL TO SHEILA MAHONEY

All too soon you left us, Sheila,
All too soon you slipped away,
But we believe that you're with Jesus
And so we celebrate today.

We celebrate the glad reunion
You must be having with your Dad;
Yes, Daddy's girl is beaming;
It's the best time that you've had.

You're singing with the angels
And I think I heard one say,
"There's a special mission for you, Sheila,
Come with me; I'll lead the way."

Suddenly you are surrounded,
As you tread those streets of gold,
With a host of furry puppies.
More than your loving arms can hold.

A reminder of your precious mother,
How she held you to her breast,
And throughout your life on earth
Gave you strength and peace and rest.

Oh, Sheila, we shall miss you;
All too soon you've slipped away,
But Praise God for having known you;
Let us celebrate today.

January 20, 2007

## A SILVER ANNIVERSARY OF SERVICE
To Carolyn McLean
Administrative Assistant, First Christian Church

A Silver Anniversary of Service
Performed by Carolyn McLean
Reveals what a wonder she is;
To be smiling and happy and sane.
Today we celebrate with you, Carolyn,
And look back over those twenty-five years,
Recalling our good times together,
Counting our blessings 'mid laughter and tears.

How many pastors have you assisted,
And filled-in when they were gone?
How many times have you held us together
When there was no one, no one but you alone!
Your service to us has been priceless;
They say the best things in life are free.
God-first in your life speaks volumes,
And it certainly has spoken to me.

You're more than a payroll worker;
You're serving your Master above.
As we work in His Vineyard together
We learn the true meaning of love.
First Christian Church wants to thank you.
Listen as they say it again,
"We celebrate all of your service;
And the whole church says, 'Amen'!"

August 20, 2006

## TO MY DEAR FRIENDS AT PROVIDENCE

I would like to thank you
For the gentle, loving way
In which you cared for my needs
With the dawn of each new day.

While my husband was a patient
It almost seemed that I was too;
I felt so woebegone and weary
And didn't know what to do.

Loving friends came to my rescue
To calm and steady me
And this heartwarming home
Offered real hospitality.

Clean sheets, hot baths,
A place to rest and pray,
But more than that warm faces
To share experiences each day.

I'll always be grateful to you
For you saved my husband's life.
And then, as God would have it,
You reached out to me, his wife.

The story of the good Samaritan
I see in what you do;
Saving souls and healing lives.
Providence, may God always bless you!

January 20, 2001

## A TRIBUTE TO DOCTOR ALLEN

Teachers are very special people,
Like gardeners, if you please,
Daily planting seeds of knowledge,
Tending their learners
With the greatest of ease.

Teachers are explorers,
Opening up their students' minds
To the joy of old and new technology
And the challenge that ever binds
Teacher and learner together.
Ah, yes, they ever seek and search
And find success
As rung by rung they climb the ladder
To Graduation and much deserved happiness.

More than a teacher, Doctor Allen,
We feel you are our friend.
We want to thank you;
We want to acclaim you,
And remember to the end
You gave to each of us
A gift the world can't take away.
May God bless you and all your graduates
On this Graduation Day!

Graduating Class of 2001
University of South Carolina School of Medicine

March 24, 2001

## STANDING ON THE EDGE OF TOMORROW

Standing on the edge of tomorrow,
Thinking of what can be.
It's like taking a first peek at Grand Canyon
Or viewing a mighty, rolling sea.
It's knowing what God can do through us,
Feeling the strength and spread of His wings,
Compelling ourselves to commit anew
To the tug which pulls at our heart strings.

It's having our Region healthy and strong,
New churches budding and Timothies too.
It's reaching out as servants of God,
Sharing and caring in all that we do.
It's dreaming and daring and planning our way,
Working together to reach our goals,
Not for prestige or power or well-deserved praise
But to bring to Jesus some searching souls.

It's thanking our Savior for where we have been
And praying He'll allow us to be
A part of His Church marching onward,
Celebrating the twenty-first century.
It's standing on the edge of tomorrow,
Holding hands with you and you and you;
For we are the church together.
Dear God, please make our dreams come true!

September 1996
Written for program booklet for
Regional Assembly of Christian Churches of SC.

## FIRST CHRISTIAN'S FIRST 100 YEARS

Here in this new millennium,
The year 2002,
We look back one hundred years
To what is now affecting me and you.
Indeed, not one of us had then been born;
Centurions we're not,
But our church had its beginning
In 1902 on a small Pickens Street lot!

Seven dedicated Disciples had a vision;
They set out with courage and with prayer
To form the First Christian Church of Columbia,
Inviting others to join them and share.
Together they built a tabernacle
And filled it with humble praise.
God used them to attain a victory
Which blessed and hallowed all their days!

In the years that came after,
And as the congregation grew,
A new edifice was constructed.
This one familiar to many of you.
It was here we brought our children;
It was here we came to pray,
And there were many celebrations
We remember to this day!

Then came the urge to move from the downtown area
To this beautiful spacious place.
In 1962 the present building was dedicated,
With God's blessings and by His grace.

Not only were we grateful for this fine structure,
Culminating the faith and efforts of our congregation,
But we rejoiced to know God's church is more than
brick and mortar;
It's joining hands and hearts in a deep spiritual relation!

Feeling that we should build again
To fulfill the dream of a Child Care Center
We completed a versatile building in 1994,
Giving ample room for classrooms and a social hall
accommodating 200 or more,
But for reasons beyond our control,
And after much work and prayer,
Sadly we closed the Sonshine Center and sold the
equipment last year.

For those who led us on this journey
We give our heartfelt thanks today.
Each in his own time contributed;
We walked in faith the pilgrim way.
But we are not through dreaming;
In God's vineyard there's always much to do.
Here on this busy boulevard, in the year 2002,
First Christian of Columbia reaches out
With a challenge old but ever new.
Will you be His true Disciples,
Chart the course of this new day.
Will you answer as He calls,
Stop, listen, follow Jesus all the way!

Written for celebration of our church's 100th birthday;
and presented January 13, 2002.

## CANE RIDGE MEETING HOUSE

To us Disciples
Cane Ridge Meeting House is a shrine.
It holds precious mem'ries of our beginning,
And stories dear to your heart and mine.

If it could talk it would tell you
How the frontier people held hope
For a practical, down-to-earth religion,
Which would ease their hard lives and help them to cope.

It would tell you of their thirst for God's word.
Once they gathered to sing and to pray;
By hundreds they came from the hills of Kentucky,
Families staying day after day.

They listened to stump preachers rant on and on,
Methodists, Baptists, Presbyterians too,
While the children played or slept or cried.
For sure it was time for their church to begin,
Time for great leaders to be tested and tried.

Barton W. Stone, Thomas Campbell and Alexander Campbell came
to the rescue
And the Christian Church (DOC) was born,
One of the largest churches founded on American soil,
An answer for the 19th Century and even now for me and you.

Today, In Columbia, we celebrate our Centennial.
How grateful we all should be
That our roots are from that little shrine.
Oh, give us some more of that Cane Ridge religion;
Lead us, oh Lord, Divine!

July 28, 2002
Written for Centennial Celebration of
First Christian Church, Columbia, SC.

## DEDICATION OF HEALTH KITS

God, bless these gifts we've brought with love,
And send them on their way.
To help the children of Mozambique
Have a somewhat brighter day.

Their lot, we know, is sad indeed,
Disease and suffering, starvation too,
Present the pictures from which we turn.
How can such horror affect me and you?

It calls us to compassionately give,
To do what we can where we are,
To feel the joy that will come to a child.
In Christ Mozambique isn't far!

It points to what our Master said,
Words that will stand for eternity,
"If you did it not to the least of these
You did it not to me!"


July 18, 2000
Written for Dedication Service of Health Kits
collected for Mozambique by
Rehoboth United Methodist Women,
Columbia, SC.

## THE CHURCH AT THE END OF OUR SEARCH

We were invited to a little country church,
A sister of ours, you know.
Come share the service, the singing, the food;
Such mingling is great and helps us to grow.

The directions to find it seemed simple enough;
Go West on I-20 for miles and miles.
Take Exit 22 and turn left and left and left.
Country roads, dusty roads, strange faces and smiles;
They, for sure, lead to somewhere
But not where we want to go.
Are we lost; is there help?
If we don't ask, how can we know?

Some never heard of Merritts Bridge Christian Church.
Others quite willingly gave another wrong way.
Finally, there was someone who knew for sure;
With time running out, he saved our day.

Well, at the end of our search there stood the church;
Yes, over a hundred years old.
Kindred spirits worship here; God seems very near.
And its message is purer than gold.

It makes me remember that Heaven's in store;
What a feast awaits you and me.
If we find the right road and follow it too,
It will lead to Eternity.


April 30, 2002

## GOD IS STILL CREATING

God is working, still creating
From the stones and from the clay
Of the earth He once created
On a celebrated day.

He is changing clay to jewels
By a process taking time.
By the pressure and the heat
He must mold your life and mine.

When the miracle has happened,
And the stones are jewels true,
How we'll shine for our Master,
How we'll love each thing we do.

God is working, still creating
From the stones and from the clay
Sapphires for foundations
Of that home we'll have one day.


October 9, 1988
Entered in contest offered by World of Poetry.
As a result, I was invited to attend
their Convention in Washington, D.C.

## COME, WE THAT LOVE OUR CHURCH
### (Sung to the tune of "I Love Thy Kingdon, Lord")

Come, we that love our church
And raise her banner high.
Praise God for these one hundred years
And hope that will not die!

Come, let us share the feast
Which speaks of His great love,
Which marks us as His children here
And in that home above!

Come, let us bow and pray
And count our blessings too.
Envision what we can become;
Let God use me and you!

Come, let us feel the joy
Of knowing who we are,
Disciples in His world today,
A mission reaching far!

Come, we that love the church
And raise her banners high,
Praise God for these one hundred years
And hope that will not die!

January 13, 2002
Written for the Centennial Year of
First Christian Church, Columbia, SC.

# FAMILY

Family is the closest thing to Heaven
That we on earth will know.
Family is the closest thing to Heaven
For God ordained it so.

Lord, bless our family.

## LOVE IS

Love is more than pretty words,
Paper hearts and dainty lace.
Love is knowing Jesus Christ
And His sweet, abiding grace.

Love is living in the sunlight
And the shadow of His Cross,
Bearing up beneath our burdens,
Smiling when we have a loss.

Love is ever climbing upward,
Though a struggle it may be,
Reaching out to help another,
And His face at last to see.

Love can hold us all together,
Mold and make us really strong.
Love can open up locked doors
And fill our aching hearts with song.

Love is more than pretty words,
Paper hearts and dainty lace.
Love is sharing Jesus Christ
And His sweet, abiding grace.

February 2, 1993

## THE THREE MEN IN MY LIFE

There are three men in my life
And they mean the world to me.
I love each one completely
And it's for all the world to see.

First, there is my darling husband;
For sure, he's one of a kind.
Pappy, I count it a blessing
That I can claim you for mine.

Then there is my handsome son
As fine as a son can be.
Stevie, I hold you close to my heart
Although you were born to be free.

Finally, there is my grandson,
Oh, Jed, how we all love you.
A man you are yet to become,
But I can see that dream coming true.

Yes, there are three men in my life,
And to each there's a wish and a prayer.
For around you is a circle of love
That grows bigger year after year.


February 2, 1990
Written on Pappy's 76th birthday and presented
at the family celebration of that happy occasion.

## LIKE FATHER, LIKE SON

When Stevie was a little boy
I knew there could not be
Another one as full of life
And like his Dad as he!

From cowboy boots to baseball bats
The days and months flew by;
The motorcycle was the thing
That often made me sigh!

But he survived and went to war,
The Air Corps sending him;
And on furlough he took a wife.
Now how we do love them!

God's richly blessed their marriage
And their precious family;
There's Stephanie and little Jed
To keep us company!

He walks beside that Dad of his
And smiles so happily;
Oh, what a pair! No doubting there,
They mean the world to me!

## TO OUR CHRISTINA

I see her as a baby,
Filling our hearts with joy,
Our cuddly, cooing first-born!
Now, who could have wished for a boy?

I see her as a lovely child,
Anxious to learn and to grow,
Feeling "responsible" for her brother,
Who made his appearance next, you know.

A pretty teenager emerges,
With a future shining bright;
Graduations and a career beginning,
She was kept busy from dawn 'til night.

Now I see her as a woman grown,
Accomplishing much in a very short time;
Diligent, talented, dependable,
This devoted daughter of mine.

But that's not all of the picture;
She's compassionate, caring, and giving;
Her faith in God is unshakable,
Spelled out in her every day living!

CHRISTINA, WE LOVE YOU!

March 11, 1996

## CONGRATULATIONS, STEPHANIE

These are the things, Stephanie,
I'm wishing for you;
Contentment and joy
In whatever you do.

The best things in life
Are waiting for you.
If you can attain them
Your dreams will come true.

We celebrate with you
Your Graduation Day,
And remember so proudly
You've come a long way.

But your learning's not over;
It's only begun,
Keep passing the torch
'Til the race has been won!

May 21, 1993
Presented to my granddaughter,
Stephanie LeAnn Stevens,
upon her graduation from Ben Lippen High School.

## TO JED UPON HIS HIGH SCHOOL GRADUATION

Because you're very special,
And because I love you too,
I'm praying that your future
Will hold great things for you.

You have the desire and the will
To succeed at what you do,
A personality to win friends
And make your dreams come true.

Whether you go on to higher learning,
Or begin a working career,
May you be blessed in your decision
And know that to me you are dear.

Upon your high school graduation,
This wonderful day of days,
I offer you congratulations.
We love you, Jed, always.


June 2, 1995
Presented to my grandson, Charles Jedidiah Stevens,
upon his graduation, with honor, from Columbia High School.

## TO MY VALENTINE

God brought us together
By His mysterious ways
That we might spend our lives
Giving Him our thanks and praise.

On Valentine's Day you asked me
If I'd become your wife,
And we've been sweethearts ever since;
It's been a love-filled life.

The past ever looms before me,
With memories I'll always hold
As treasures to leave my children,
Treasures more precious than gold.

Retirement has become our portion
And grandchildren to bless our days.
Hand in hand we continue our journey
In the strength of God's wonderful ways.

Valentine's Day now finds us
Somewhat slower, even limping along,
But our hearts are still young and singing
A long-ago, faraway, sweetheart song!

February 14, 1989

## WILL YOU BE MY VALENTINE?

Snow was lightly falling
On that evening years ago,
Giving a glow to our nation's capital,
My home, for how long I did not know.

These were the days of World War II,
Uncertain, frightening, full of youth and love.
Families were torn apart each day
As prayers of hope and trust went up to Heaven above.

We stood there waiting for the trolley,
Music of Naughty Marietta still ringing in my ear.
Suddenly you drew me close and whispered,
In fact, so softly I could hardly hear.

"Sweetheart, I love you, will you marry me
And always be my Valentine?"
Now each February I remember
And thank God such memories are mine.

I thank God for our lives together.
Hearts and lace we know are only frills;
It's love for home and friends and one another
That brings to us the everlasting thrills.

February 14, 1996

## TOGETHER

Together we've shared our lives,
The months, the moments, the years.
There's been a world of happiness,
And sometimes a time for tears.

Our children have been our jewels,
Adding a sparkle to mundane days.
Together we're serving the Lord
In many and varied ways.

Our grandchildren are the spices;
They're cookies and ice cream and more.
They're what we've always wanted.
My goodness, how did we live before!

But you are the special one;
Pappy, this is your special day.
Together we are a family.
God, keep us forever we pray!

Happy Father's Day.


June 18, 1989

## HAPPY BIRTHDAY, PAPPY

Of all the birthdays we've celebrated
This one is the best.
No cake, no party, just quiet peace and rest;
But how we rejoice together
And thank our God above
For the long way you have come
Through medical expertise, patience, prayer and love.

You're a hero, Pappy.
We know you fought to live
Because you felt within your heart
You had something more to give.
You've made so many people happy
Just to know you as a friend;
And, of course, my life is you, my love,
And will be to the end.

So on this very special day,
When you are eighty-seven,
Let's count our blessings one by one
And feel we're close to heaven.
Happy, Happy Birthday!
May you have many more!

Love,
Mommy

February 2, 2001

## HAPPY BIRTHDAY, PAPPY

Today is Pappy's birthday
And he is ninety years old.
There is warmth in the cards and greetings
But the weather outside is cold!

Nevertheless, he's out there
Working away at the wood,
Getting it ready for another winter.
Who, but he, would do it if they could.

He seems propelled by a motive
To do all that he possibly can,
And no one can stop or deter him
Because he's a strong-willed old man.

Don't stop him; just help him;
He knows what he wants to get done.
He also knows he is happiest
Working from dawn to setting sun!

Happy Birthday, Pappy!
May you have many more!

Love you,
Mommy

February 2, 2004

## FIFTY YEARS OF LOVING

Love is whispering wedding vows
By flickering candlelight.
Love is starting life together
With visions of a future bright.

Love is waiting out the war years
With letters, cards and gifts,
Working in the nation's capital,
Long hours, long prayers; God lifts.

Love is meeting deadlines
And paying all the bills,
Welcoming the little ones,
A home, a hearth, a dream fulfills.

Love is worshipping together
And serving in God's fold,
Sharing the fellowship of believers
And the greatest story ever told.

Love is reaching the golden years,
Retiring from professional work,
Finding time for little things;
Some responsibilities to shirk.

Love is looking into your face
And knowing you still love me.
Time has not changed those long-ago vows.
They were made for eternity.

Happy Fiftieth Wedding Anniversary!

May 1, 1993

## ANOTHER WEDDING ANNIVERSARY

Another year together!
We count so happily
The third one from the golden one,
Our fiftieth wedding anniversary.

Another year together!
We count our blessings too;
How good, dear Lord, you've been to us.
Our praises rise to you!

We thank You for our years together!
You've made our bond so strong
'Twill last through our remaining days
And be our farewell song.

Our children will remember
The love song of our day.
May it be the anchor of their lives
To keep them loving you, I pray.

HAPPY ANNIVERSARY, PAPPY.


May 1, 1996

## OUR 55TH WEDDING ANNIVERSARY

The months and years have passed so swiftly;
I can hardly believe we're old.
But time has not changed our thinking;
Our love still shines like gold.

We come and go and work together;
Life is so sweet these days,
A simple routine, but God is good.
He's blessed us in many ways,

Surrounded by friends and family,
Who really love and care,
And time on our hands to do as we please
On this happiest day of the year!

And what do we do to celebrate?
The thing that seems easy to do,
Helping at church, lending a hand,
Just knowing He loves me and you!

Happy Anniversary, Pappy.


May 1, 1998

## OUR 58TH WEDDING ANNIVERSARY

When I look back across the years
To May 1, 1943
My mind is filled with happy thoughts
Affecting you and me.

We've scaled the heights together;
We've known both joy and pain.
We've felt God's hand upon us
Like sunshine after rain.

I thank God for His walk with us,
His guidance for each day,
Assurance of life's rainbow
When we hope and trust and pray!

We celebrate this span of time
God gave us graciously.
With humble, thankful hearts we mark
Our 58th Wedding Anniversary!

I love you, Pappy.

May 1, 2001

## HAPPY ANNIVERSARY, PAPPY

Fifty-nine years is a long time indeed,
But you know it seems just yesterday
We stood at the altar and said our vows
On that beautiful first day of May.

You were a soldier of World War II,
And soon you'd be "shipping out."
Time was so precious to us then;
To be together was what marriage was about.

After fifty-nine years we can truthfully say
That statement still is true.
Lord, please grant us a few more years together
Is a prayer for me and you.

Happy Anniversary!

I love you!
Mommy


May 1, 2002

## OUR 60TH WEDDING ANNIVRSARY

How long have you been married?
Again this question comes to me.
To tell the truth, it seems forever,
Not just our 60th anniversary.

I pause to think how time has passed,
How mem'ries fill our book.
Now blest we are to celebrate
In our quiet little nook.
No fanfare needed, no bells to ring;

We're happy just to be;
For we've known love and have not lost.
This is our victory!

Happy Anniversary, Pappy!
I love you!


May 1, 2003

## OUR 61ST WEDDING ANNIVERSAY

A cross-stitched pattern comes to mind,
One that is close to my heart;
It's the picture of a small wedding
In a little chapel set apart
From the busy, hurrying world,
Just made for you and me;
Because we were the happy couple
Saying our vows for eternity!

The pattern reflects the times
Of sixty-one years ago,
And yet they are the same as now:
War and love; together they flow;
Couples snatching some time together
While awaiting the overseas blow.

Oh, how we longed for peace!
Oh, how we watched for a letter!
Oh, how we prayed each day
And worked and planned
For a future when things would be better!

Oh, God, we truly thank you
For making our dreams come true,
For connecting all the little stitches,
Changing the skies from dark to blue.

Now wrinkles and backaches
Do not change the picture
Because it was designed by Him above.
It is a cross-stitch of His making,
And is a reflection of His love.

Happy 61st Wedding Anniversay, Pappy.
I love you!

May 1, 2004

## 62 YEARS TOGETHER

Sixty-two years together;
Now that's the story of you and me;
Of a marriage that has survived,
And will until Eternity.

Time has a way of passing;
So it doesn't seem that long
Since we were young and singing,
Dancing to a sweetheart's song.

You've given me candy and flowers;
You've given me gifts galore.
You've given me love and a home.
Now could anyone wish for more?

You've given me mem'ries I'll never forget.
I'll always hold them in my heart.
Such is the way our lives have been
Always together and never apart.

Happy Wedding Anniversary, Pappy.
I love you.

Mommy

May 1, 2005

## PAPPY'S QUILT

Imagine all the countless hours
That are cross stitched here.
Imagine how each block became
A picture bold and clear!

Imagine all the love expressed
In color and design;
This must match and that must blend,
Just like your lives and mine.

Imagine as the years go by
What an heirloom this will be
And always a reminder of
The dear one we call Pappy.

Imagine how much joy is ours
To present this on your Wedding Day
With love to Stephanie and Archie.
God bless you both, we pray.

May 27, 2000

Dear Stevie,

Since you were a babe-in-arms
I have held you close to my heart,
And you have returned that love
In so many ways.

You are strong like your father,
Dependable and wise.
God-fearing, affectionate,
And to the world's eyes
You're a leader, a manager,
A special sort of guy.
But to me you're my Stevie
And my, oh, my,
I love you more
As the years go by.

Happy Birthday.


August 20, 2006

## CHRISTINE

Christine, you're always doing
something to brighten up my days,
You're there when I need you,
And in so many ways
You seem more like a daughter
Than it's possible to say.
Please know that I love you;
Have a Happy Birthday!


March 25, 2007

## TO JED AND CHRISTY

I remember when you said your vows;
How radiantly happy you seemed to be.
Yours was a story-book romance;
May it last for eternity.

Happy Wedding Anniversary!

Love,
Gran Gran


May 3, 2007

## MY FIRST GREAT-GRAND

She's a darling; she's a doll,
A long-time dream come true.
Olivia Anne, you're our princess;
With love we all crown you!

We hope you'll grow, as babies do,
Step by step and day by day,
Until you stand before us,
God's blessing for our pathway!

And in the years to come,
When Great-Gran is no longer here,
Remember that a legacy of love
She's left for one so sweet and dear!


Olivia Anne Stevens
Born to Jed and Christy Stevens
July 22, 2009

Dear Christina,

It's been a long, hard year for all of us
Especially, for you and me
But it has brought us closer
And made me know
How strong we each can be!

Together we've faced problems
And solved them one by one.
Now if I were totally alone
What would I have done?

So on your special day
I want to thank you
And pray this special prayer,
God bless and keep you always
In his eternal care.

Happy Birthday!

I love you!
Mama


September 9, 2006

## WHEN HE CALLS

When He calls us
We must answer,
Here I am Lord;
I will go;
I will serve You
Where You need me;
Teach Your children,
Watch them grow.

China seems no longer foreign;
For we've found true friendship there,
And we know we have
Your blessings
And the love of all that's here.

Gracious Father, walk beside us;
Help us in the tasks we do.
May our lives be filled with joy
As we live each day for You!

August 2005
A tribute to Archie and Stephanie Stevens Crossland,
who are returning to China as teachers for the new school year.

## WITNESSES FOR CHRIST

We are called to serve Him;
Each in his own way.
To teach, to preach,
Or just to humbly pray.

It may be distant China,
Or another foreign field;
But when we receive the nudge
Then our hearts must also yield.

Difficulties face us;
There is no rosy bed;
But Jesus walks beside us.
By Him we're daily led.

Yes, we are witnesses for Christ,
And we never count the cost,
For we know we will be richer
If we prevent one soul from being lost!

June 22, 2006
Written for Archie and Stephanie Crossland,
who are serving as missionaries to China.

## LITTLE GIRLS TOGETHER

We were little girls together,
Having our pictures made,
All dressed up for the occasion
But without a smile, I'm afraid.

We were pouting about a basket
The photographer had given to me.
"You can't have it; it's mine, Vondelle."
That's logic when you're still not three.

Oops! There goes something on the floor,
Running fast and shining bright.
At that moment, flash, goes the camera.
Now our expressions will come to light.

We were little girls together,
Playing in the sand;
With all our woes behind us,
Life was simple, sweet and grand!


June 24, 1999

## OUR MOTHER

When we were little children
She led us by the hand
To this dear place of worship
That we might understand
The joy of knowing Jesus
As Savior, Lord and Friend;
The One who is our Shepherd
Even to the End!

In Life she walked before us
In an humble, upright way,
Forgetting self and helping others,
As a motto day by day.
In death she's still our guardian
And keeper at the door
From which she now is beckoning
With that smile she always wore.

Good-bye, dear Mama,
We shall miss you.
Life can never be the same,
But we know that you're with Jesus
And we bow and praise His Name.
In the quiet of these moments
We would thank Him up above
For a life so nobly lived,
For a gentle mother's love.

Written for the memorial service for my
dear departed mother August 19, 1974.

## MY MOTHER

She gave me life;
She gave me love.
She taught me wisdom
Comes from above.
She walked before me
In a righteous way,
Scattering sunshine
Each new day.

She was not rich
In things on earth,
But just her smile
Held so much worth.
People loved her;
'Twas easy to do.
Her prayers were a magnet,
So earnest and true.

She's finally Home,
Where she longed to be,
Leaving only her love
For a legacy.
Dear Mother, dear Mama,
My teacher and friend,
You're still my shining star
And will be to the end.

March 19, 2001
My Mother was Mrs. Roy Franck of Sandy Run, SC,
a devoted member of
Beulah United Methodist Church of Sandy Run.

## MY SISTERS

I have three living sisters,
Who mean so much to me.
They connect me with the past
And a beloved family.

We did not have great riches
But we were taught to share;
In doing so we learned a lesson,
How to live and love and care.

As we've applied this logic
To our living day by day
We've found joy and contentment,
A peace the world can't take away.

I have two departed sisters,
Whose mem'ry I revere;
They're shining stars in Heaven
To bless and call me there.

## WHAT THE SCARECROW SAID

First, let me say I was made by someone special
For a person who was special too.
He thought everyone was special
As he shared the vegetables he grew.

I am the keeper of his garden,
Mr. Stevens' garden, you know,
Ah, yes, I watched him as he worked,
Patiently tending row after row after row.
Often I wanted to talk to him,
To tell him a secret or two,
But he was always so busy.
Now what could a scarecrow do?

They tell me I was made to scare crows;
Well, bless you, I never saw one,
But the deer! How they came and they plundered;
They trampled and nibbled until there was none.
Mr. Stevens was discouraged,
Especially when they ate all the peas;
But he never gave up; he had high hopes
As he toiled down there on his knees.

He had high hopes for the sweet potatoes
Now growing so healthy and green.
The deer had high hopes too
And they ate 'til no leaf could be seen.
They tell me Mr. Stevens has gone up to Heaven
And left me to keep this dear spot.
Well, I'll do my best as a scarecrow;
You bet, I'll give it all that I've got.

September 24, 2005

## BW

I'm really not a cat lover,
As my dear daughter is,
But BW says I'll change all that
And the expertise is his.

When I walk out to mail a letter
He follows close behind,
And as we return he capers,
Doing stunts, if I don't mind.

When I sit outside on the deck
He begs to rest upon my lap.
Oh, well, I know he's weary;
Why not take a little nap.

You'd never know we're only neighbors
And that he's my daughter's cat.
With a loving meow, meow, meow,
He says I've changed all of that.

With a sense of caretaking,
Beyond his aging years,
God's creature teaches me a lesson:
Love gives, forgives, and forbears.

March 10, 2007

## JASPER AND JERRY

Jasper and Jerry are friendly dogs.
They, too, are family, you see.
Different in nature and in looks
But congenial as they can be.

Jasper has always been in charge;
He knows he's the king of his home.
Jerry came when his folks went to China;
So he's humble, obedient, not anxious to roam.

Jerry is afraid of thunder;
He whines 'til there is no more.
Jasper is afraid of nothing;
He sleeps and you might hear him snore.

Ah, but a noise awakens him!
Not thunder, but a truck or a car.
To the window he bounds and announces,
"Someone is coming; stay right where you are!"

If that someone's his master or mistress
He's excited as he can be.
There's always a royal welcome
Worth a million bucks to see!

March 10, 2007

## OUR DARLING DUCK

If ducks could talk she'd tell us
Of the experiences she had
When we thought we had lost her
To a sly old fox or bandit bad.

The pond was frozen over,
And ice was everywhere;
So we think she lost her bearings.
Oh, she must have been filled with fear!

Over the dam she wandered,
Slipping and sliding along.
We don't know where she went,
But we missed her quack-quack song.

We missed her at feeding time;
We missed our beautiful pet.
White like the snow of the winter,
She was belle of the duck jet-set.

With warmer days upon us,
And dreams of coming spring,
The grands went out exploring
To find 'most anything.

To their surprise and ours,
They found our darling duck.
Wow, what a celebration!
Could this have been sheer luck?

If ducks could talk she'd tell us,
But we're glad to have her back.
There with her family on the pond,
Gliding along, Quack, Quack, Quack, Quack!

January 31, 1988

## 85 YEARS OF BLESSINGS

Eighty-five years of blessings
Have brought me a wonderful life;
Now a mother and a Gran Gran,
More than sixty years as Pappy's wife.

I gave my life to Jesus
When I was a little girl,
And promised I would love Him
More than anything in this world.

There's a verse in the 91st Psalm;
This Psalm is a favorite of mine.
It says He'll cover me with His feathers,
A security, I feel, no less than divine.

His truth will be my shield and buckler,
A strength I have found to be true,
As I've leaned on this eternal rock,
Finding joy with believers like you,

Loving and serving go hand in hand.
Praise God for the innumerable ways
We can love Him and serve Him
Through a lifetime of hours and days.

Eighty-five years of blessings
The Lord has given to me.
My prayer, dear Father, is that they reflect
My gratitude to Thee!

August 19, 2003

## THIS DIGITAL AGE

When you're approaching ninety
And living all alone
Don't dare relax your thinking
And feel you're almost home.

There're many lessons you must learn
And put them into use;
Mechanics, electronics, horticulture,
environmental control,
Estate planning, legal scanning.
It sounds like real abuse!

Whether you can see or not
Read the fine print on the page
And follow all instructions.
This is the digital age!

July 22, 2008

## HEARTS AND HANDS

Hearts and Hands is a group
Whose mission is to share
The literal message of our Lord:
To lift, to love, to care.

Every blanket that you make
Becomes a blessing true.
A little one cuddles in its warmth
And smiles his thanks to you.

Perhaps you'll never know the names
Of those who get these gifts
But rest assured you are remembered
By Him who knows
and loves
and lifts!

Keep up the good work, Hearts and Hands!


May 1, 2010
Christina is a member of Hearts and Hands and
contributes generously to its ministry. The founder of the group,
Charlene Pankow, says Chris is a virtual quilting machine.

## PAPPY STEVENS AND HIS WALKING CANE
### (HERMAN C. STEVENS)

We called him Pappy;
What an endearing name,
And of equal interest
Was his old walking cane.

Inseparable companions,
Sturdy and sure and fleet,
The cane kept him from falling,
Giving him confidence on his feet.

It was created by him
From a random cherry bough,
One of the many things he made;
We don't know exactly how.

We miss this Christian brother,
The tap, tap of his earthly cane.
Though his footsteps are forever silenced,
We'll meet him in Heaven again!


June 7, 2006
The men of our church made a glass case for Pappy's cane
and asked me for a poem, which is beautifully framed.
These hang in our large social hall as a reminder of our love
for Pappy.

## PAPPY'S GARDEN

Pappy's garden was his pride and joy;
Indeed it was his favorite niche.
Laboring there contentedly
He felt so satisfied and rich.

Connected with his world of nature,
He watched the seeds he planted grow.
He thought the birds sang sweeter there
And saw the honey bees blessing every row.

When harvest came 'twas time to share
With friends and neighbors too.
I think that God has truly smiled
Upon this gardener true!

Now he's with the angels
But somehow it seems to me,
He's also here in his garden;
Each blossom testifies so beautifully.

March 22, 2007

## A MEMORIAL TO MY BELOVED

Sweetheart, husband and very best friend,
God gave us a love that will never end.
He brought us together in Washington, DC,
Lonely young hearts, yes, you and me.
You were a soldier, that sergeant I knew,
Serving our country in World War II.
I was there as a civilian, doing my share,
The beginning of a long civil service career.

We were married in spring, the first day of May,
A memory I cherish unto this day.
We said our vows without much fuss,
But we felt God was listening and blessing us.
What really mattered was the time we would share
Before you were called to "come over here."
That call came sadly in early fall;
It was hurry, get ready; you can't drop the ball.

Two years passed before I would see
You coming home and sweet victory!
Of course, letters and presents came constantly
To let me know you were thinking of me.
Today I remember the life we shared,
The joy that was ours; we loved and we cared.
We gave priority to God and His ways,
And He led us gently all of our days.

Our family reflects your character strong,
The jewels God gave us as we went along.
Christina, dear daughter, beloved son, Steve, and wife Christine;
You're precious to me, on you I must now lean.
Our grandchildren, too, mean so much to me;
Stephanie and her Archie, Jed and his Christy.
I must go on living but I don't know how
To God's will I must humbly bow.

At night I can hear you calling to me,
"Come, Mommy, oh please come and see.
There's a garden here in heaven
That is to be mine;
Plenty of moisture and God's sunshine.
I'll never get tired and I won't be sick,
And I'll walk like you without my stick."
Tears on my pillow and poems in my heart
Say, "Pappy, I'm coming and we'll never part."

Friends, you've come to honor this wonderful man.
Your presence speaks more than anything can.
God's humble servant; how you loved him too.
On behalf of my family we want to thank you.
God bless this church and may it ever be
A beacon that brings many souls to Thee.
To find nurture and growth and strength for the day.
In the name of our Savior these things we pray.

September 6, 2005

## FIRST CHRISTIAN'S CHIMES

What could be more beautiful
On any given day
Than the clear, sweet call of chimes
To help us on our way.

What could have more meaning
As a very special gift
To our beloved church.
Each heart they're sure to lift.

They'll give and give their message
To this community:
Jesus is our Saviour
And He can set us free!

Now as we pause to remember
One who loved this message true
We dedicate this memorial
From our family to you.

Pappy, if you're listening
From your home so high above
Please know these chimes remind us
Of your faithfulness and love!

Note: Steeple chimes of First Christian Church,
Columbia, SC, dedicated to the glory of God and
in memory of His humble servant,
Herman C. Stevens on November 2, 2008.

## TO WELCOME ANNA LUCILLE CROSSLAND

Anna Lucille! What a beautiful name!
Surely your life will be the same;
Filled with God's goodness,
Dreams coming true.
These things and more I'm wishing for you.

Like your father and mother
May you always stand tall,
Reach for the stars,
Never doubting at all.
He'll stand beside you;
He'll hold your hand
And the dreams you are dreaming
He'll understand.

From one who loves you very much,
Your Great Gran Gran


March 4, 2010

## CHRISTINE'S SPECIAL TALENT

Christine is a person of many talents
But this one took me by surprise:
She makes adorable baby bonnets
To frame wee faces, enhance their eyes.

Now that she's a grandmother
Nothing can please her more
Than to sew for her two granddaughters;
Then come knocking on my door
To share her latest success with me
For sure, I am as happy as she!

May 2, 2010

## TO ALINE COGGINS ON HER 100TH BIRTHDAY

I have a dear cousin; her name is Aline.
She is a miracle; that's plain to be seen.
Her life's full of stories; with us she could share
Times not forgotten, a family so dear!
The eldest of ten, she mothered the rest;
Helping Aunt Mamie, putting love to the test.

In time she was married to a very swell guy.
'Twas a match made in Heaven; they saw eye to eye.
God gave them two sons; they knew they were blest.
Then came cancer; her love laid to rest.
Now a young widow, she worked and she grew;
Each day brought its problems and blessings anew.

Time marches on; we find ourselves old,
But we cherish each day as if it were gold.
Few of us come as far as Aline;
One hundred years with a record so clean
She'll sing with the angels one of these days.
Hallelujah! Happy Birthday!
May God be praised!

We love you, Aline!

March 21, 2010

## MY TOMORROWS

You, Lord, hold all of my tomorrows
In the palm of Your Mighty Hand,
And I feel a sense of expectation
In a mystery I can't understand.

But when I turn and look backward
Over the span of many long years
I can see how You've guided my life,
Making rainbows of trials and tears.

I'll wait for the shadows to pass, Lord.
I'll labor and love and pray;
I'll keep on looking for rainbows,
The kind that will last for aye.

I'll walk in the sunlight with you, Lord;
I'll follow You all of the way.
I want You to be my Companion
Minutes by minute and day after day.

For You hold all of my tomorrows
In the palm of Your Mighty Hand,
And I feel a sense of expectation
In a mystery I can't understand.

March 2, 2006

# ABOUT THE AUTHOR

✦

Caroline Franck Stevens was born in the Sandy Run Community of Calhoun County, SC, August 19, 1918. She spent her childhood there as a member of a loving family of eight (five sisters plus Mom and Dad). In her senior year of high school her English teacher requested each pupil write a sonnet; so Caroline wrote her first poem. The teacher noted Caroline's efforts at writing and encouraged her to continue on this magic journey. The Great Depression deferred any ideas of college; after a business course and a few years in the working world, Pearl Harbor caused major changes to be made. Accepting a call to begin a long civil service career, Caroline found herself removed from the routine of a sleepy little SC town to our busy nation's capital. After living there a year, she met the love of her life, Sergeant Herman C. Stevens, and to her great joy, he wrote poetry too.

In the years following their marriage, when Herman served our country in England, France, Belgium, Holland and Germany, many poetical love messages were exchanged. After two long years victory came and Herman returned to the good old USA. The happy couple took up their abode at a gold mine in Montana, where Herman had a job waiting for him as a mining engineer. Their first child, Carol Christina, was born there a year later. Herman C. Stevens, Jr. would be born two years later in SC, where they returned to live (in a warmer climate) and Herman became employed by the State Highway Department as a highway engineer. Later, Caroline took up her civil service career again at Fort Jackson, SC, retiring from there with almost 30 years of service and then doing a stint of almost seven years with the SC Department of Mental Health. Together Herman and Caroline retired in 1981, beginning a long and happy segment of their lives. These were the golden years, a time for gardening, crafting, traveling and yes, writing poetry. Their days were filled with work and contentment. Up until a few weeks before his death on Labor Day of 2005, Herman continued his duties at church and plodded to his garden every day.

The church has always been the center of Caroline's life. She has served in various duties: more than 30 years teaching primaries; CWF leader, Shepherd, Elder, and Poet Laureate. She has been a member of First Christian Church (Disciples of Christ), Columbia, SC for almost 62 years. Her writings are colored by her faith in God, love for family and friends, experiences of a happy marriage of more than 62 years, the wonders of nature, the tug of a little one's hand, the glory of an Easter sunrise service, the joy of hard work and accomplishment and sweet dreams.

Caroline lives alone in her country home at Blythewood, SC, but has family and great neighbors close by. She has two children, two grandchildren, and two great-grand children.

LaVergne, TN USA
26 September 2010
198503LV00003B/2/P